Ina

Thank you Imes
infinity —

xo Stacey

Stacey Zisook Robinson

Dancing in the Palm of God's Hand

Reflections on meaning, faith and doubt

Hadassa Word Press

Impressum / Imprint

Bibliografische Information der Deutschen Nationalbibliothek: Die Deutsche Nationalbibliothek verzeichnet diese Publikation in der Deutschen Nationalbibliografie; detaillierte bibliografische Daten sind im Internet über http://dnb.d-nb.de abrufbar.

Bibliographic information published by the Deutsche Nationalbibliothek: The Deutsche Nationalbibliothek lists this publication in the Deutsche Nationalbibliografie; detailed bibliographic data are available in the Internet at http://dnb.d-nb.de.

Coverbild / Cover image: www.ingimage.com

Verlag / Publisher:
Hadassa Word Press
ist ein Imprint der / is a trademark of
OmniScriptum GmbH & Co. KG
Heinrich-Böcking-Str. 6-8, 66121 Saarbrücken, Deutschland / Germany
Email: info@hadassa-wp.com

Herstellung: siehe letzte Seite /
Printed at: see last page
ISBN: 978-3-639-79420-5

Dedication

To my beloved son, Nate, who has taught me everything I know about the holiness of doubt, the grace of struggle, and who dances with me in the palm of God's hand.

To my family and friends, who have shared their questions and strength, their stories and hope; who have caught me and carried me when I couldn't find the path on my own; and who celebrated with me always - thank you for your light and love.

Table of Contents

Dedication 1

Introduction 7

Faith 10

In-Betweens and Almosts 11

A Lesson, Learned Again 13

Rowing Towards Shore 16

Good Intentions 19

In Praise of Doubt – 21

The Sound Between the Notes 22

The Perfection of Belief 24

Platespinner 29

A Matter of Faith – and Monkey Bars 33

Song, Unfinished 36

Soft Landing 41

Nothing More than Feelings 44

The Holiness of Broken Things 48

Faith Enough 52

Hope Stronger than Fear 55

The Music of God (Part 1) 56

The Music of God (Part 2) 60

Hope Enough to Share 64

Boxing with God 66

God of the Ocean 70

Epiphany at the Gas Station 73

Chasing Fireflies 77

Anniversary 79

Simple Stories 81

The Empress of Forever 84

Faith and Meaning 87

Choreography in Holy Time 88

Time and Light 91

Fringes 94

Joy in the Empty Spaces 97

A Quiet and Holy Current 99

A Cry in the Wilderness 102

The Sound of Your Voice 104

Blessing and Pain 107

Who Brought Us to This Moment 109

Shabbat 110

Week's End, with a Promise 110

The Holiness of Separation 112

Psalm 92 114

Friday Night Kitchen 116

And When I Leave 117

Passover 119

Fear, Faith and a Really Big Sea 119

Opening the Door 122

Counting the Omer 125

The Holiness of Silence 125

Shavuot 127

What I Brought 127

Tisha B'Av 130

An Absence of Color and Light 130

Rosh Hashanah 133

In the Space of *T'kiyah* 133

Chanukah 137

War 137

Bound to Freedom 142

Mourning 144

Ribbons 144

Twenty Three 146

Mindfulness 147

Be 148

Believe 149

Bless 151

Clean 153

Count 155

Dare 157

End 159

Enslave 161

Fear 163

Forgive 165

Hope 167

Justice 169

Learn 172

Leave 174

Mercy 176

Peace 178

Pray 180

Ready 182

See 184

Trust 186

Understand 188

Wonder 191

Endings and Beginnings 193

Return 194

Epilogue 195

   More Questions than Answers 195

Copyrights 198

Introduction

I am a Jew by choice.

And before you ask - both my parents are Jewish. One of my earliest memories is being with my grandfather, sheltered by his *tallit*, as he gave the benediction to the congregation on Rosh Hashanah. We celebrated most of the Jewish holidays with a meal. Occasionally, we even made it to synagogue. My parents helped found the first Conservative synagogue in the south suburbs of Chicago, and my dad served as its first president. I started Sunday school as a young kid, and Hebrew school in third grade. The first word I learned was "*b'vakasha*" ("please") - I remembered it because it had four syllables. It was probably the longest word I knew at the time. The first song I learned was "*Hinei Mah Tov*." I sang it incessantly.

I was educated as a Jew, the full complement: Sunday school, Hebrew school, bat mitzvah and confirmation classes. I was dropped off, sent inside while my parents had a quiet Sunday morning, or a free hour in the late afternoon on Tuesdays and Thursdays. I sat, every Saturday morning for almost a year, reading ancient Hebrew and what seemed like even more ancient English, littered with "thees" and "thous" and flowery beyond belief, alone among a handful of old men, as required by the dictates of the Ritual Committee and my upcoming bat mitzvah. Alone, because my parents had other things to do.

I devoured religious school. I felt as if I had come home, had found the place where I belonged (had always belonged), the familiar and sheltering *home,* as we navigated through Jewish history and holidays. I ran through all the primers for Hebrew that our Rabbi could throw at me, so that by the time we switched synagogues and affiliations joining the Reform synagogue a year or two before my bat mitzvah, I was a year ahead of the rest of the kids in my grade.

There was youth group and music. Debbie Friedman's (*z"l*) songs grabbed something inside, got our hands clapping and hearts soaring. We sang a new song to God, and did it with joy.

When I became a bat mitzvah (although, when *I* became a bat mitzvah, we still *had* a bat mitzvah; there was none of this "becoming" stuff), from the *bima* (think: pulpit), as I gave my bat mitzvah speech - I declared my parents to be Lox and Bagel Jews - people who ate their way through Jewish culture, but who, when push came to shove, really felt more comfortable on the golf course than in the sanctuary on a Saturday morning. I further declared that I would never be like them (remember, I was a teenager). Most important, I declared my intention, my desire, to become a rabbi.

All of my fervent declarations were met with a hearty chuckle, most especially from my parents. Although they were willing to play along with my more participatory adventures in Judaism, they drew the line at the Rabbinate. "That's really not a job for a nice Jewish girl," they told me. Funny thing, it had nothing to do with the fact that I was a girl - after all, we were living in the modern world of 1974, and women could do anything (sort of). No, they didn't think the calling appropriate because they figured I'd never make enough money in praying professionally.

Like most teenagers, I was adamant, intractable, supercilious and superior. At thirteen, I knew the answers to life, the universe and everything.

By fifteen, I knew that there was no God and that religion - specifically Judaism - was nonsense. I refused to participate because I refused to be a hypocrite. Of course, I still took off from school, and later, work, for all the major Jewish holidays, and ate all the major Jewish meals at their appointed times, each in its season. I mean, really - a girl has to eat, right?

I did not set foot in a synagogue again for many a decade.

Between my late teens and my early forties, I was a Jew by birth, and that's about it. I did not disavow my Judaism, did not seek other religious options (though I flirted with alcohol as an emergency spiritual path, then a kind of universal (not Universalist) just-be-a-good-person, kind of peace-and-love amorphous spirituality that had no form, and certainly no God). It was easier for me to be disconnected and contemptuous, and so I was.

And now? Now I am a Jew by choice. Every day - let me repeat that - *every day* I choose to be a Jew. Choose to engage and connect and participate and act and worship and pray *as a Jew*. It is a conscious act, like the King who says to Scheherazade: "Good story. I guess I won't kill you today. Maybe tomorrow." Some days, I am the King; some Scheherazade. I must both *act* and *choose*.

Getting to this place, for me, was a long and twisty road. I lost a lot of things along the way, but I found more than I lost. I found a measure of peace, a sense of wonder, the joy of obligation and the freedom of service. I found God - and danced and wrestled and rested with Him. Her. Whichever, whomever - the God who chastised and punished and redeemed and loved. The God of Abraham and Sarah, of Miriam and David, of Spinoza and Rashi, the Baal Shem and Shabbatai Zvi. And woven betwixt and between this heady God, was the God of my grandparents, Irving and Jean and Morris and Yetta. Justice and mercy, compassion and love, and I learned to stand on the shoulders of giants and find comfort in my questions and doubt.

I am a Jew *because* I act. I am a Jew *because* I choose.

Today, I choose faith. Today, I choose doubt. Today, I choose to struggle and question and learn and sing and pray. Today, I choose to dance in the palm of God's hand.

Faith

The place where God lives

I find my faith and my God in my breath. My faith changes – it shrinks and grows and moves and dances. I have to work at it. If I am honest, I often have to be reminded of it – of my faith and doubt and breath. The essays in this section celebrate the grace of the reminder, the in-rush of breath, which brings movement and change and letting go.

I am caught -
And I am carried -
And I climb
This ladder of light.
And there,
At the center -
At my beginning,
At my end,
Which is all of me -
In that place,
I dance
In the palm of God's hand
And I am whole.

Selah.

In-Betweens and Almosts

The ancient Celts had the right idea: it is in the in-between that magic lives. Dawn, not daylight; dusk, not night. Who would have felt the enchantment of Brigadoon if it lay under the bright golden summer blue sky? It was in the very fact that it lay shrouded in fog and mist that we could believe in the magic of that place. There is an expectancy, an urgency that goes with that in-between and almost time.

In-between is all about possibility. It is the infinite and unknown. It is Schrödinger's Cat living large. Or perhaps dead. Or both together. It is where God lives, in the space that exists between me and you. It is magic and mystery and enchantment.

I am fascinated by the in-between, by the infinite.

I just wish I could *do* them. I wish I could fit in that space. I have an impossibly difficult time with it. While I sense the majesty and magic, can feel the Almost gather its shape, I feel all lopsided and clumsy and wonky. I do not know how to respond. What I crave is knowing what will happen next. I want the rules, dammit. I want to know what's expected of me. Don't make me guess. I do not know how to relax. I cannot sit comfortably in the dynamic tension of in-betweens. I feel it much like a cat or dog feels the tension of a coming earthquake: disaster is just around the corner and I want to bolt before it hits.

And right now, my life feels ruled by the twin novae of In-Between and Almost.

Panic, pure and simple. It is uncertain and twisty, the path that lies at my feet. There is hidden quicksand, I am sure of it. I cannot see all the traps; there are shadows and menace and probable monsters. There is endless despair and eternal night. It gets worse. I crawl inside my head to escape this uncertainty and the tensions magnify.

My skin buzzes, my foot jiggles, my thoughts skitter, making up the eleventy-seven thousand stories that go along with "what if..." In the absence of information, I make stuff up. It is never of the happily-ever-after variety. In my stories, the evil wizard triumphs over good, the dragon eats the princess, and the hero gets lost in the woods. And that's the beginning of the story; the end is not nearly so upbeat.

But here's the thing: even in the midst of my panic, there is a grace note of something else, something that may almost be hope. There is this poised expectancy, like the ghostly breath of God that hovers over a field of grass at dawn, waiting for a single breath to give it shape and movement. That is my life: poised, motionless, waiting for a single breath to give it shape. And my instincts scream: run!

But I don't. I don't run. I stay waiting, skin crawling, watching and waiting for what happens next. It can drive friends and lovers mad. I, myself, am an in-between and an almost. I am neither here nor there. I flit and twirl and dance along a razor sharp path to get over the endless chasm of almost.

Relax. Let go. Let be. Just be. Wait.

Do they all not understand, even now, what I wouldn't give to be able to sit in comfort and quiet in the magic of that in between? Do they not know how glorious it would be to breathe and just be?

And I can almost get it. I can almost find that place, poised so exquisitely between the infinite and the possible. And that is the whisper of hope. I am almost, I am in-between, and I can breathe. Just breathe. And the wonkiness, the twisty anxiety, they give way, with infinite slowness, to the beauty of almost and in-between. And I can sit still, and wait, and go slow: for a moment, a breath, a day, some finite time where I don't have to know.

It is where God exists. It is where love resides and hope is born. It is redemption and grace. It is the place of my heart. Even in my fear, even in my panic and uncertainty, I am given these gifts.

And I find peace.

A Lesson, Learned Again

I have this picture in my head, of what it looks like to have faith. It is me, standing on the edge, right at the top of some impossibly high mountain, the sky a deep cerulean blue, luminous and rich, the air crisp. I stand, poised, ready to leap, to soar and fly and float and land, without doubt, in absolute certainty, to rest gently in the palm of God's hand.

I do a lot of standing.

Faith is tough for me.

I *want* to leap. I want to have that certainty. I want to rest with God, be carried through. I want it desperately. Sometimes, I feel it, a tiny trill of anticipation tweaked with fear and nerves and excitement, radiating out weakly from my center. Fingers and knees tingle, and for a moment, just a moment, the barest whisper of a moment, I gather myself and breathe and

Stay. Stuck. Wistful and regretful. And safe.

Sigh.

Like I said, I *want* to leap. Sometimes that level of faith is just beyond me.

And yet...

And yet, every once in a while, I soar.

And when I do, I find God's hand, outstretched, waiting for me. Every time. Without exception. Every time I leap, there is God, waiting for me.

I wish I could remember that, that God waits. Just for me. Always. Patient, comforting, with a hint of the eternal. I don't though. I stay, wrapped in my doubt like a blanket, sure (sure-ish) that fear and doubt are safer than that split second of free fall until I find God's warmth. I hear the echo, ever and always and first, of the only prayer I had for a couple of decades: "Screw you, God." I wrote that prayer at a young age, sure that God had abandoned me, had left me to struggle in pain, to drown in my loneliness. I declared my apostasy loudly - "There is no God!"

Of course, the louder I shouted, the more I could drown out the whisper that slips so softly in my head, the idea that, it wasn't that I didn't believe in God, it was my undeclared certainty that God didn't believe in me. It was *that* certainty that kept me rooted, poised and still. I cannot leap, because I am afraid that God still has His (Her?) back turned away from me.

No redemption for you! Ha!

And yet, I have leaped and soared and slipped gently into the ever-present outstretched hand of God. My struggle, my disbelief, my lack of faith is just that: *mine*. My holy and sacred quest is a shadow dance, and God is enthusiastic spectator in that solo performance. God watches, applauding my every effort, laughing in all the right places, waiting for me to lose myself in the moment.

It is not *what* I pray. It is *that* I pray. That's what matters. That's what makes God dance.

I was at a retreat. It was possibly all about music. Or maybe about prayer. Or God. Or community. Faith, perhaps. All of the above. Certainly, music was the base, a foundation of sorts. Shabbat Shira - Sabbath of Song. A few dozen people came together to learn and stretch and grow and teach. Silly me; I thought I was there to learn more about song leading - using music and song to lead congregants in prayer. Simple stuff.

Ha!

What I learned was all about love, and community and faith. Yes, faith. That damned elusive *thing*, that spark of God and hope that I chase with all the singularity with which a drowning woman chases a life preserver floating just out of reach on a dark and wave-wracked sea. Throw in a bit about vulnerability and truth and honesty and you have the weekend. Our teachers stood before us, offering themselves, whole and pure and unafraid, without pretense, and made a glorious noise as they lit a path to God. I followed. We all did, joyously, surrounded by love and faith and hope.

How? I asked. I demanded. I pleaded. How do you do it? How do you show up, vulnerable and raw? How do you give? How can I?

And really, that was my prayer. My quest had gotten me this far: from "Screw you" to "How can I?" I *want* to serve. I *want* to give. I want to be an unsheathed flame, dancing along a path to God, letting others in to find their own paths, their own joy, their own prayer. I want to leap. *Please God, let me leap*. One more time, let me learn the lesson of soaring. Let me believe that I will be caught.

And my teachers, every one of them, whether they stood in front of us in service or beside me in prayer (because everyone at Shabbat Shira was my teacher), they all answered so simply, so stripped of artifice: *you just do*.

It is not what you pray; it is that you pray.

It is not what you do, it is that you do.

It is not what you sing; it is that you sing.

Do. Act. Pray. Sing. Serve. The grace (and gracefulness) will follow.

The widow who joined us on a GNO (1st for her) told Marianne: you find a love like that when you are willing to give 100% of yourself – like jumping off a cliff, knowing he'll catch you.

Rowing Towards Shore *... I am responsible for rowing"*

Pray to God, but row towards shore.

I do a lot of praying these days. Not so much on the rowing. I seem to be a bit stuck. Sigh.

Don't get me wrong - I love the praying part. I get lost in the praying part. It's like finding a thread, maybe even that elusive blue thread, out of the corner of my eye, that one beautiful thread that allows you to dance along its very narrow edge knowing that a single misstep that would cause you to fall, to be lost forever - but the joy of it, the grace of that dance is enough to carry you, with surety and ease, straight to God.

Like I said, I love that dance, and I get lost in it. But here's the thing: I don't just use that dance, that praying part, as a refuge, a safe haven in a restless, roiling sea of life, where chaos licks at a shore that is pocked and unstable, eroding faster than, well, sand in water. I use it to hide, to keep from rowing. I pretend, fingers in my ears and "la las" spilling from my lips, louder and louder to reach over the growing crash of waves that threaten to fill my tiny boat and sink me, I pretend that praying is enough.

I forget, oh-so-conveniently, that I am responsible for rowing. You know the story, right? There once was a man, gentle and mindful and good, who was devoted to God. Prayed all the time. Practiced compassion and was righteous and kind. One day, while on a cruise, there was a horrible accident and this man ended up on a deserted island. The man, though, had the absolute strength of his faith, and knew, without a doubt, that God would save him. So he prayed. He prayed day and night, mostly echoing the tender, plaintive words of Moshe: Please God, save me. He felt a little uncomfortable, praying for his own redemption, but he knew that his wife and children and friends needed him, his employees needed him, and his clients and the community needed him. So he prayed.

On the second day, in the middle of his morning prayers, the man heard the distant drone of an airplane. Soon he saw it flying not far from his little island. So he prayed harder, "God, please save me!" The next day, as he prayed, he heard the sound of a ship's horn, sounding loudly, not too far off, but he refused to be distracted from his prayers. "God will save me, I know it!" Soon, he could only hear the sounds of his own prayers; the boat missed the island and continued its search for the man in other latitudes. On the third day, the man's prayers, softer now, as he was hungry and thirsty and nearing death, his prayers were interrupted by the thwap-thwap-thwap of a helicopter. The man, filled with the fire of his belief in the saving power of God, refused, again, to be distracted by the annoying interruptions around him, and he prayed all the more diligently.

On the fourth day, the man found himself in heaven, standing before God - Creator of All Things, the Merciful Judge - and he scowled. Scowled! Oh, he was angry. "God!" he cried. "God - I have been your faithful servant, a good man. I've followed your commandments, provided for my family and my community, worked for peace, fought for justice. My faith was strong. And when I needed You most, You ignored my most heartfelt pleas! Why didn't you save me?" His anger gave way to his pain.

God looked at the man with infinite love and compassion. "But I sent you the plane, the boat, the helicopter..."

I sit in my boat, praying like mad, staring at the shore and willing it to come to me. I tell people that I am working to perfect the Telepathy App. They think I'm joking. I mostly am, but there is that small part of me, that little kid part of me - the kid with the pigtails and shiny Mary Janes, who is sitting on the swings, motionless, staring at the playground full of kids, willing them - wanting them - to come near, to be next to, to care - that little kid is desperately praying: "You do it. I can't. Please."

There are times - days, months, eons that become concentrated into a single instant - when I cannot act. I can only sit, watching life and the shore and the playground with utter longing. But I'm scared, and lonely and less than and vulnerable. I pray and pray and pray, but the oars absolutely defeat me.

In my posed and poised position, I wait for release. For change. For movement. I forget, in the midst of my prayer, that it really does begin with me. Pray with your feet. Doesn't have to be a huge and boundless leap into the great unknown. A step. A single step, no matter how small, that step moves me forward.

That is where faith lives. That is the beginning of redemption and the saving grace of God - a single step, from here to there. I am called upon to act. Through the fear and shame and guilt, and whatever else keeps me stuck and sitting alone on that swing, I must ACT. And in that action, no matter how infinitesimally small, that movement carries me closer to God and closer to you.

Pray to God, but row towards shore...

So, why pray? for what?

Good Intentions

I had intended...

Wait. Let me start again, this time in the present tense. I intend...

Ugh. I have no idea what I intend, what I had intended, what I will have intended.

What I know is that I love the English pluperfect tense: past, present and future, all rolled into one. I am a grammar wonk of the highest order. Even more than the English pluperfect, I love that, in Hebrew, we consider not necessarily past, present or future, but perfected versus not perfected. Action over time, complete versus intended.

The holiness of completion and the grammar of intention.

They are intricately – intimately - connected, by time, by action, by desire. It is not enough to want. It is not enough, even, to do. The rabbis tell us that in order to satisfy a mitzvah, I must have intended to do so. I must consciously perform the act or the action or task or I will not have satisfied the commandment.

I strive for completion, for the mindfulness of my intention. I intend to fully engage, in my Judaism, in my continued and continuing conversation with God, in finding a path to wholeness that shelters me and the world entire.

My Intentions mostly support this. My actions, though, can be - incomplete. I am subject to the laws of unintended consequences. My grammar can be faulty in this. I am less than holy though, I am human; no more, no less. I have hurt others, through my thoughtlessness. I have been unkind in my haste. I am unforgiving in my passion and self-righteousness. I am cruel in my fear. I am cynical in my doubt. I do not intend to be these things. My intentions are (mostly) good. Please God, don't let me be misunderstood - least of all, by me.

One of my favorite of the midrash is one of creation. There are ten things, the Rabbis tell us (except when there are seven) (or thereabouts; depends on the text, the rabbi, and the midrash you read) (because the Rabbis can spin many plates at the same time, and there is always room for one more)-- there are ten things that were created before God ever created the world. Depending upon where your finger lands in the text, these included the rainbow, and the burning bush and the ram's horn. Some include things like manna or Miriam's well that sustained us in the desert. The greatest of all of these, though, to my mind, is the creation-before-creation (don't get me started on the grammar of that, or its tense!) of *t'shuvah*[1].

How awesome is God! How great is the Creator of All, to know that there would be a disconnect between intent and result? How breathtakingly, achingly divine, to understand, before creating the heavens and earth, we humans would need a path back, a way to return? We will sin, we will fall short, but we will not be abandoned. The gates of *t'shuvah* will always be open for us, whenever we approach them, whenever we get up the courage to walk through.

Be holy, we are told, because God is holy, and we are made *b'tzelem elohim*: in the image of God. But we are human, and so, for all our mindfulness, for all our drive towards completion and wholeness, we will fall short. We will hurt the people we love, we will be indifferent to the needs of others, we will turn away the stranger in our midst, even when we intend otherwise.

Just as God intends for us to find the way back, to return, to stand, once again at the Gates that are thrown wide (or opened only a small crack) - we will find forgiveness, we will find God, we will find each other, ever and always, there at the Gates. And in the very instant that we step through, in that breath, that heartbeat, that intention - there is neither past, nor present nor future. There is only wholeness.

The holiness of completion, the grammar of intention.

---

[1] Return, redemption

In Praise of Doubt –

Faith, Doubt and Belief

Doubt and faith and belief are inextricably linked for me. They create powerful and prayerful moments that allow me to find connection and a glimpse of God. And as much as I'd like to say that I always make it to that place, sometimes I get only as far as the hope of it, and that has to be enough.

I find God in my doubt,
In the struggle to Be
The absolute best of me,
And in my fear
That I find only my
Worst.
I wrestle,
and am restless
and I wander, rootless,
exiled,
barricaded by my silence.
God of Hosts
and Light
and Mercy -
God of the desert
and unseen edges -
God of my devotion
and my rebellion:
Open my lips
That I may declare your praise.

The Sound Between the Notes

There's a cacophony of noise going on in my head, a clanking clattering collection of caliginous junk that sets my teeth on edge and makes my skin buzz. There are a thousand conversations happening, about everything, all at once. Or about nothing, all at once. A thousand? Sometimes it's ten thousand. Sometimes it's infinity. The sound swells and recedes like the ceaselessness of the ocean. I can't remember the last time my head wasn't filled with sound.

I would really like for the noise to stop.

That's a wish pulled from the depths of my earliest memories (and trust me - I have a memory bordering on the freakish, that could be compared to elephants and the madmen who carry grudges and fan the fires of blood feuds and even bloodier vendetta): please, just make the noise - that dull, droning, sub-vocalized, just-at-the-edge-of-hearing noise that sets your teeth on edge and your skin buzzing - make that noise stop. Please. That may be my wish, perhaps my prayer. Thing is, I've never been quite patient enough to wait. I've never been trusting enough to believe that my prayer would be answered (at least, not answered with a "Certainly, Stacey, coming right up!"), or my wish granted. I've always felt the need to help it along. *Taking responsibility*

And help it I did. At least, that was the plan. I threw everything I could at the problem, mostly none of it healthy. Addiction is an insidious creature, whispering of a redemption bought with the currency of self-destruction. One more seductive voice (in an ocean of voices) added to the chaos in my head, and I chased that siren song with desperation-tinged despair that I could have sworn was hope.

But that was long ago and far away. Right? Right?

Still a wish. Still a prayer: please make the noise in my head stop. And I still step right up, to fix it, all on my own. And every time I shoulder the burden of my own prayer, all I manage to do is turn the amps up. To eleven.

God, but it's noisy in here. It's a maelstrom of sound and I am drowning in it. Writing helps, some. Singing, too. And prayer. I still have a few dark and twisty places inside, so that my manic attempts aren't always quite so healthy as that. They all tamp it down, make it less whinging and relentless, bring some melody to the disparate notes I hear. That I always hear.

"... the whispered brilliance of the sound between the notes

All I do is hear, ceaselessly, endlessly without respite. And all I want is quiet, a moment of silence, a chance to breathe, to think, to be. Just be.

I say this, pray this, desperately hope for the grace of this. And all the while, I harbor a secret fear. And sometimes, the noise in my head is loud enough, all echo-y and whisper-y and discordant and driven by my ghosts -

I am terrified of silence.

I am afraid to get that quiet: quiet enough so that I can really hear. Really hear the sound of my heart, the song of my soul, the music of God. To be still, to be quiet, to hear - myself. To hear my hope, my despair, my prayer. And then to wait, in quiet stillness, to hear God's answers. To let the fear go, in my quiet, that there will be nothing there, a cavernous, echoing silence, to realize, in fact, that I am alone.

I surround myself with noise - a great cacophony, a glorious, messy din, so that I can avoid hearing my fear. I avoid the breathtaking beauty of silence. But here's the thing. The glorious thing, filled with wonder and light: For a minute or ten, every so often, there is this awesome - not silence, but, I think, but quiet. It doesn't last, mostly. I blink, or breathe, or maybe I just don't pay attention enough, don't nurture that calm and quiet enough, Or maybe I do too much, and try to hold it captive, like a butterfly pinned to a black velvet board, and so we're back to cacophony. Sigh.

But for all of that, I get glimpses. I hear the whispered brilliance of the sound between the notes - and it is there that God's voice lives.

And into that glorious stillness, that in-between space of holiness and God, I will say "amen."

The Perfection of Belief

I set out to write something profound, some lyrical piece of prose that weaves a myriad of disparate threads into a single and vibrant whole that creates a luminous and holy path to belief.

I want to bring you to the mountaintop, so that you can feel the presence of God, find that transcendent arc that allows you to dance in God's hand. I want to hear that sigh, of relief, of recognition - *yes; this is it, this is what I believe, this is good.* Like coming home after a hard journey, not to fanfare and parades, but to warmth and love and gentleness.

What I get, more often than not, is a heavy use of my delete key: pixels scattering through the ether, getting eaten by the very hungry ghosts in my machine. What I get, more often than not, is doubt.

Belief can be hard.

It feels so much like walking on a high wire without a net, belief does. It's a precarious perch, and I hate to admit that, after decades of mindful searching, I find I misplace my belief almost as often as I find it. Dammit - why can't I have what Maimonides proclaimed: *I believe with perfect faith...*

What I have learned - slowly, *very* slowly - is that my belief is a living thing: it grows and recedes and changes. What I believed as a child has changed. Thank God. Back then, I believed some pretty weird things, not least of which was that magic was real, unicorns lived and my baby brother was part chicken because he had to live in an incubator for a while after he was born (long story short: he was *not* part chicken, though he was jaundiced). As an adult, I can ask: What belief *hasn't* changed?

There was a time I did not believe in God.

There was a much longer (and more desperate) time I believed that God didn't believe in me.

There was a time that I didn't believe in myself. This is still true. Sometimes.

There was a time I believed I was broken, unfixable, irredeemable. That's the thing about belief: it changes. It deepens, softens, drifts in an ever-shifting pattern.

I take a breath of time to challenge my beliefs, to be mindful of them, to examine them in the light of day and under cover of star-bright skies. When I look close enough, I can see, woven among the thousand, thousand strands of my belief, doubt and cynicism and naiveté. My disbelief is there to be challenged just as well.

Finally, I understand: It's all good - my belief, my doubt. It is neither black nor white, the world of my belief: it is a bright and shining place of glorious silver. I don't need to be like the *Rambam*; I don't need to believe *perfectly*, I just need to believe.

Filled Enough

Um.

Excuse me, but, uh, this is not the life I ordered.

Not even close. Not by a long shot.

As a kid, there was the vision of the Astronaut Life. The Broadway Mega-Star Life (with a side order of Rock Star, although I'm not sure which was the real expectation and which the fall back). There was a brief (though infinitely more serious) flirtation with Rabbi, Writer, World-Shaper and Doctor (of philosophy, not of medicine). Teacher was up there, too.

And those were just the professions. There was also the Wife-and-Mommy Life (in that order; I'm kinda old school that way). That one wove its way in and under and through all the rest - International Jet Setter; Nobel Peace Prize winner; Solver-of-All-Problems-and-Healer-of-All-Hurts.

And through it all, in every dream and desire and expectation - Happy. Loved and loving. Sitting comfortably in my own skin, sure and confident.

Somewhere along the way, my life took a left turn. And then a right. And then a few squiggly hairpin turns that curved in on themselves until they teetered on the edge of the scary mountain pass that had no guardrails or pavement. And then the road disappeared altogether, into the swampy underbrush (and yes, I do realize I'm mixing metaphors here, or at least describing an impossible geography that can exist only in my head; I'm okay with that).

My life is infinitely messier than my expectations.

I find that the disconnect between my expectations and the reality that is my life feels somewhat akin to that steady, thrumming drone that gets just under your skin, that makes me buzz and my thoughts crackle. It is the dissonance that I feel, that I almost hear. It makes me crazy, this peripheral insistence of disquiet.

For decades, I would view my life out of the corner of my eye, willing it to fit the mold of my expectation. Willing, scheming, manipulating - some weird and twisted Machiavellian plot, I was determined to make the square peg of my reality fit into the round hole of my expectation. Or something like that:

some distorted and disproportionate plan to smooth over the cracks that spider-webbed across my universe of one.

Have I mentioned my flair for the dramatic?

God, but I'm exhausted.

I am tired to the bone, and I have missed so much of my life! I have been focused on some Siren call, urging me ever onward to fix and manage the life I have - the one I wake up with every morning, that is lumpy and tangled and dull and lonely and fine, really fine, and every once in a while, filled with aching beauty and breathtaking wonder. And yet, I will pass that one over in a heartbeat, and trample it in my eagerness to make it happen: the right life, the chosen life, the better life.

You know, the life that would make me happy.

If only you would -

If only I could -

If only everything would just - .

I'd be happy then. Wouldn't I?

And the lesson learned, again and again (or, not learned exactly, so that I could move on to different things, but at least a lesson experienced, again, and yet again): it never works, this attempt to turn fantasy into reality. All effort to the contrary (and oh! I expend a monstrous amount of effort in this impotent pursuit!), I just get more empty, starving on a heaping serving of subtraction stew. The more I take, the more I pound, the more I want, the greater the disconnect grows.

Here's the strangest thing of all, though: there is grace, even for me, even in this. There is hope. I have felt it, sipped at its intoxicating sweetness and relished its exquisite simplicity. Acceptance. That's the answer. Really: just show up and let it be. Life will happen, in all its glory. And I will be there, not out of the corner of my eye, not as some third rate puppet master, but as me, present and alive.

What an awesome and simple and excruciatingly difficult thing that is!

The cynic in me wants to sneer - that's not simple, that's naive and dangerous. Why, anything might happen!

Well, yes, anything might happen, and often does.

And so I come full circle, and am reminded, as I so often am: this is the lesson. Let go. Let be. Let life happen, be filled with wonder and boredom and sadness and laughter and disappointment and hope. There are a thousand things and ten thousand more that can happen, that can fill you - but you will be filled. Filled and full, and your life, at last, will be enough.

Platespinner

Call me Platespinner.

Like that guy who ran around the stage on the Ed Sullivan show, to keep the thirty-seven five-foot tall dowels spinning in mad counterpoint to the music, all to keep the plates that lay on top from toppling.

Manic. Frenetic. Exciting.

Exhausting.

No time to think: just act. Keep it all spinning. Forever.

Call me Platespinner. Welcome to my life.

I don't remember a time that this hasn't been the metaphor for my life. Some people have theme songs; I have a metaphor. And ok, I probably have a theme song, too, but that's a subject for another time, a different essay. Because this is all about -

This is about -

What I'm trying to say is -

Here's the thing - *Why are there so many fucking plates spinning on top of those damned spindly dowels, for God's sake?!*

Who the hell put them there? And what the hell do I care if they spin or not? And why, God - God of Infinite Mercy, God of Sneaky Irony, God of Whatever Thing You Want to be God Of - why do I never once stop to question why I keep adding plates to this unholy mess? *Seriously*. Even *this* has become merely a new plate to spin, and it *already has* become lost in the forest of all those other naked dowels. Just add one more to the pile. To the pyre.

Because at some point, this forest, this pile, it all becomes a pyre, and those flames will burn hotter than my guilt and shame put together. They will skip and dance up to heaven itself, and carry me - consume me - along the way. And I just keep adding more fuel. And more plates, over and over.

There's work stuff and Nate stuff and house stuff and God stuff. There's carpools and repair shops and therapy for me and grocery shopping and what do we do about Mom and did you remember to pay this bill and what about that library fine and you promised we could, you said that I could and have you talked to Dad lately and can you help with homework? And can you bake for this? And can you fix that other thing? Can you talk - write - pray - sing - do - run - drive - go - cook for me? For them? Just a little? Just this once?

And that's just the *Stuff* stuff. The tip of the iceberg, everyday, ordinary stuff. That doesn't even come close to the other stuff - the Dream stuff, and the Fear stuff and the Hopes stuff - all those things you put into all those boxes labeled "Pandora." Mostly you keep those lids on pretty tight, but every so often, almost like that scab that you just can't quite leave alone, you pick at one, just a crack, and out slips - something.

All those Dreams you had, of becoming something – someone – great. Or maybe that secret fear, that really is mostly just shame dressed up into something so much finer, that you thought you had conquered *last* time, but there, in the dark, when you're tired and maybe a little lonely and, ok, let's face it, cranky, which you'd really like to blame on the hormone thing, but, if you had to be honest, it really is that you're angry - out creeps that shameful, dressed up fear. It crawls out of the box and up onto a plate, spinning now like a whirling dervish, and singing at the top of its metaphoric lungs.

And don't forget your Hopes. For you. For your son. For your friend, and your friend's friend, and the teacher at the school and the person whose name you forgot, the one you see all the time at synagogue, who is kind and says hello after services every week - who's been struggling some lately, whose mom just died, whose dog is sick and her husband got laid off and left and what hope is left for her? And, of course, you can't forget your hopes for the world, and all the starving people who seem to multiply daily and the poverty that threatens to drown entire countries, and maybe even continents, in endless, insatiable need, and all the oppressed people, and the dolphins and baby seals and bees. What the hell is happening with all the bees, and what the hell are we going to do if they all just die off? Who is going to fix that?

Have we hit thirty-seven plates yet?

Without breaking a sweat.

I breathe, and six more plates pop up, seemingly of their own volition. *And I never once stop to question why, God, why do I just keep adding plates.* I never once stop to ask what would happen if a couple dozen of them came clattering to earth, scattering into shards and dust and broken, jagged pieces.

And right now, this very second now - there is nothing left. The field is full. Screw the plates and my insane drive to keep them all spinning and unbroken. If I try to put in one more dowel, add one more plate - no matter how fine and delicate the pattern - I will break.

This has happened before. I live my life, spinning and whirling and running as fast as I can, gathering up plates and piling up stuff and sealing boxes that keep cracking at the seams, just moving until I am lost, and moving for the sake of moving, mindless and driven by all the hounds of hell. There's no reason, other than to keep it all in the air.

Because I can. Because I must.

I am the Fixer of Broken Things. I fix. I heal. I mend. I do. And I do. And I do. No help. No questions ever asked. No hesitation. No pause. Fix it all. Take it all on. Take it all in. Alone. Because you hurt. And you need. And you want. And you ask. All for you. And please don't confuse my frenzied action with selfless sainthood! Good God. It is all self-preservation! Because if I can fix you and mend you and focus on you, then I don't have to look at me.

Because I could do it all. Because I didn't need anyone. Because asking for help meant being less-than and wrong and horribly, painfully vulnerable. Because that's when the white hot pokers came out, looking for all the soft spots. Because I would rather die than admit that I needed help.

Because I knew I *would* die if I asked for help.

Because I knew, way deep down, that if I asked for help, it wouldn't come.

So you breathe. And you breathe again. And you add a plate; then another, and another and another. Just pile 'em on, do more, run more, breathe and gasp and stumble and spin and spin and spin. Keep spinning. Just keep it all going, more and more, until you're bowed and bloody and broken. And then you just - do more.

Until it all comes crashing down. Until you are buried under the weight of your failure and your guilt.

Please God, you whisper, *no more.* Please. And you ache and you twitch, like an addict desperately seeking - and hopelessly dreading - her next fix, you tweak and you sweat and you crave, actually *crave* setting up the next plate and setting it into motion. It is your motion of the Heavenly Spheres, perfect and glorious and deadly in all that vast and empty space.

Please God, you whisper into that dark and dangerous place, *please; I am so tired. Please - can I stop now?*

And you wait. And you listen, straining past the breaking point to get an answer, that it's okay to stop, to rest. To just let it all go, plates be damned, because the world will spin on its axis without any help from you. And you feel as if you could die from listening so hard, and your body is fairly thrumming with the effort, and your chest is about to explode because you haven't actually taken a breath in a while.

And it is silent. And it is cold and lonely and vast.

One more plate. Just one. Promise...

But what is the intent?

A Matter of Faith – and Monkey Bars

I am stuck. Really, really, really stuck. The cemented-in-place kind of stuck. You know what I mean – the kind of motionlessness that you used to get when you were a kid, sinking low in your seat when your teacher asked a question, laser eyes searching through the sea of desks, looking past all the waving arms, all the eager faces demanding attention, demanding they be given their chance to show off and shine. And of course, the teacher looked past them, *through* them, looking for You, the one kid who so did not know the answer, flop sweat soaking through your shirt and making your skin clammy, where you begged silently, "don't see me, don't notice me, pass me by, *pleasepleaseplease*," knowing that if you even *thought* about motion, you would be caught, noticed, called on to answer that unanswerable question. So you made yourself small and held yourself still. Unmoving. Willfully stuck.

And you got called on anyway.

I don't like being in this place, this needy and scary place. I want to be in control, captain of my life, captain of happy. I was talking a friend, who told me that the only thing left for me to do was to ask for help. Not from a person, but from the Universe. God. Whatever I might choose to call that thing that is bigger than me, outside of me. She said it was now a matter of faith.

Too many people are talking about faith to me these days. And it's not as if these folks are regular faith talkers. In fact, they're not. I can mostly depend on them to not talk about faith. More, I can mostly depend on them to not remind me to act on my faith. So what gives? Is this God's little joke on me? Am I getting what I need, even when I want anything but? And where is my faith? I had it just a while ago. I was floating on it, sustained and strengthened by it. It is so much easier to depend on faith when life is good, isn't it? It is the question I have been asking my Sunday school kids for years – how do you approach God in the face of joy? In the face of despair? And everything in between? I thought I had answered this question, dammit. I thought I had learned this lesson. I could have sworn I had had my long dark night of the soul, years ago.

So my friend said that this was about faith. And asking for help – but asking differently. And she said that it was okay to not know the lesson I could be learning.

But it's still scary. It still seems so large and consuming.

I hate that she may be right.

I am so used to being alone. I am the strong one, dammit. You learn, cynically, that help doesn't come, that there is no knight in shining armor and you're no damsel in distress; mostly you learn that you're alone in your need and hurt. And then you get stuck, trapped in this endless loop. So you just stop asking, because the pain of being alone is always greater than whatever need you have that's driving you to ask for help.

I am the Fixer of Broken Things. I slay the dragons and exorcise the demons and forge paths and light torches. For others. I do not get healed. I don't know how to ask for myself. I don't know how to say I am in need. I get wrapped up in the story of stuck, of the big and scary stuff. I don't always leave room for the other stuff – the small stuff, the happy and good stuff. I need to be reminded to talk about the things that are surprising and filled with grace. The things that have made me smile, that took my breath away because of their beauty or their simplicity.

So what is my good stuff? Because I need the reminder that life is not quite as heavy as I make it, I must remember the stuff that awed me or made me laugh. The stuff that got me out of my head, because I can set up camp there, live in a burnt out slum there, where I regularly mug myself. It's about faith, right? And this is part of that expression: there is good stuff in the universe – there is light and hope.

There is faith, faith enough to carry me, comfort me. Faith greater than my fear. Maybe. Perhaps. I am willing to believe that possibly, my faith is enough. That if I reach out my hand, leap into the chasm, I will be caught and held. Cherished and loved. That this dark and cold place, silent and singular and solitary, this is illusion, smoke and mirrors that are shattered with a single laugh, a kind word. I am reminded, in my faith, that it is enough to go to God and ask for help. My prayer does not change God; rather, it changes me, and my heart.

So tonight, I will act as if. Some people, some cynical people who live in my head, who like to dress all in black and smoke cigarettes off in the corner looking disdainful, they would call it pretending, not acting as if. But they would be wrong, damn them. They would be bitter and unhappy people. They would not wear their hair in pigtails and swing from the monkey bars. They would not know how to laugh; they would merely snicker.

So tonight, I will act as if and laugh and swing from the monkey bars. I will act as if I live in that bright and centered spiritual place. I will act as if I am happy and unafraid. And in my darkness, I am shown, in surety and faith, that my fears, real and scary and looming large and all-consuming, that they are made of cobwebs and dust motes. And I breathe; I move, with infinite slowness and subtle grace. I move, and it's okay to not know, to ask for help. I am not alone. There is God. There is a light. There is hope.

Song, Unfinished

There are very few things that I will admit to doing well. That is, that I will admit to doing well without a whole lot of arm-twisting and cajoling, all the while secretly loving all that arm-twisting and cajoling.

I mean, let's face it: it's kinda nice, when people argue your merits for you, to you. Sure, some of those people are family, so they almost have to (even in those weirdly dysfunctional families that are tangled and messy and just a little bit nuts; they still (at least in public) sing your praises and claim connection to your talent). Others are mere acquaintances, some casual, others less so, who say these nice things because, surprisingly enough, they just may be true. No one is holding a gun to their heads, and they don't seem motivated by blackmail or ransom. Nice.

But I do admit, pretty freely, that there are a couple of things I'm good at.

Writing is one of them (she says with only a small amount of knowing self-deprecation). I am in love with words. Have you ever watched a little kid learn a new word? You can almost see how they taste the words, roll them around in their mouths to make sure they feel right, taste right. I try to do words that way when I write: they can be so succulent, juices sweet and tart and running down my chin so I have to slurp them up, and forget using napkins or even my sleeve, it's skin-on-skin to catch every drop of them. When the word is right, it tastes like dusk in summer, or moonlight on snow. It is apple-crisp and bursting and whisper-soft, all at once. It fits, and I will go to any length to find the perfect word, to craft a perfect sentence.

I am awed by the raw power of words. Whoever first uttered the phrase "Sticks and stones may break my bones but names will never harm me" was a liar of the first order. Bones heal. Words *wound*, which is infinitely more cruel. They fester and ooze and corrupt. They kill, if not the body, then surely the soul. And yet, they have the power to heal a heart and change the world, and create joy and celebration.

Writing helps me to understand who I am and live a very examined life.

And if writing helps me to learn about myself, if it helps to keep me honest and grounded and connected to the world at large (and my life in particular), then singing is the thing that helps me to fly, to crawl outside the boundaries of my own head and find God. It is holy and sacred and transcendent, in a way that writing, for all its power and glory can never be.

It is no surprise that, somewhere in my fledgling adulthood, deep within my angry and existential angsty period, when my search for spirituality and meaning more often than not led me to a drink or six, that I gave up the two things that mattered most, that helped me to find myself and God. And believe me, this was a conscious and deliberate decision on my part. Abandoned by God? I'll show You: I will deny You (as I was denied). I will reject You (as You rejected me). *"I will never sing again,"* I said deep inside my heart, *"I will not write."* And I didn't, not for two-and-a-half grueling and lonely and desperate decades.

I was trapped in my own head, a tiny universe of one, silent and solitary and dark as fear.

It was a bad couple of decades. Getting sober helped. Having a child unlocked so much. Day after day of searching and seeking and hoping, the darkness slowly got brighter. Finding others along the way, others who offered their own illumination and could help point the way, they helped. It all helped; it was all balm to my hurt, but I was not healed.

And then one day, after my long, self-imposed exile, I walked into a synagogue. More surprising: I asked if there was a chance to sing. I didn't know I was asking to have my life changed. I certainly didn't realize I was asking to be healed, or made whole, or find God. I got all those things: in that instant, all my unasked-for yearning was answered. I found something, through my voice - through music and song - that I didn't know was possible. I certainly didn't know it had been missing. I found a connection to God that was startling in its simplicity. It was prayer and forgiveness all at once.

What began as an off-the-cuff question became an avalanche of joy. I learned how to dance a path to God, to celebrate and sing a new song. More (and here's the wonder, for me): I learned how to help others find their own path to God. It wasn't easy. It meant learning to be vulnerable, letting people in, not always singing the prettiest note, but rather the most honest one. It meant showing up, unafraid, and allowing myself to believe - even if only in the moment that I sang - that I could be redeemed, that I would be forgiven. When I did that, however falteringly, however much I stumbled along the way, I blazed a trail strewn with a light that all could follow and so sing their own songs to God, find their own voice of forgiveness.

If I sound all noble and charismatic, forgive me. It isn't like that at all. A little wonky, sure. A bit God-centric, absolutely. I was like a kid who'd just been released onto the playground after a long confinement: I wanted to feel the sun on my face and swing my arms and race the wind - and take everyone along with me. It was all energy. It was all glorious, joyful play. *"Come sing!"* I shouted. *"Come play with me! Oh! What fun we will have, all singing and praying and laughing together!"*

And they came. Not everyone. Never *everyone,* but many did, to my astonishment and delight. And it wasn't all just me; far from it. Leaders and followers - we exchanged places in a stately dance, again and again, sometimes a smooth and studied legato, sometimes a quick staccato rhythm. It was fluid grace and joyous celebration and intense, prayerful wonder.

The more I sang, the more I sang my prayer, the more I found God. Found me. Found *you,* and my place *with you,* the place that I fit, that I belonged. I was home at last.

And then one day, quite by surprise, I couldn't sing anymore. Couldn't find my voice, sing pretty. What had been effortless was suddenly strained. What had been unthinking beauty was now spotty and intermittent. My heartfelt prayer, my connection to God and grace now dust and shadow.

I had a friend once, who prayed with his guitar. That was his voice. You could see, when he prayed, when he cradled his guitar to him, made it sing and cry out, made it laugh and weep and whisper and shout, he became incandescent, a light of sacred beauty. And when he set his guitar aside for a time, when the silence of his nylon strings filled the sanctuary - you could see how that silence filled him as well. What light had flared so brightly, shining into darkened corners and weary hearts, guttered and dimmed? I was so sad for him, for us all, who were denied that spark of holiness that each of us has, not for ourselves, but as an offering to others. I was so sad that he could not find his voice without his guitar, varnished wood and nylon and metal, slim-necked and faintly worn paths that fit his fingers so perfectly, tuned to the music of the spheres, an altar upon which to place his prayer.

[handwritten in left margin: Hadn't she sought silence]

[handwritten note: But he had found his voice]

Sad, yes, and so hurting for my friend. And so secretly smug (I admit now, shame-faced), because I had my voice. I could pray without music; my very prayer *was* music. As I said, to anyone who would listen: "At first, I came so I could sing. In time, I came so that I could pray." It was *all* prayer, all praise, all holy and sacred. And I sang, and raised my voice, and found the spark and made the offering and shared the gift and sang and soared and danced and was filled.

So now, I cannot sing. How, then, can I pray? How will God hear my voice without the music that carried it - without the music that carried me? This was my gift - not that it was given to me, but the thing I had to give, my offering of thanks and gratitude. This was my salvation, a small bit of grace that illuminated the wilderness and filled it with sound.

How can I pray into this silence?

How can God hear my song when the notes are trapped inside my head?

I do not know the lesson I am supposed to learn here, if there even is a lesson. I don't believe I have a God who tests me. My God, of infinite kindness and compassion, of endless grace and gentle forgiveness, waits for me to cry out in the darkness. This I believe. This I know. But I cannot cry out in a voice that feels so broken to me, sounds so strange. On the willows there, I hung up my song; how can I sing in this foreign land?

So I stumble along, into this new-found silence. I feel quite lost; desolate and weary, and desperate to sing a song unto God that will be pleasing, that will reach God's ears.

I don't know if I have lost my song forever, if this is permanent. But perhaps I should stop searching for the familiar notes, the well-trodden pathways. What I need is a *new* song. Not for God; God hears the music between the notes, the songs our souls sing, and is gladdened by it all. Perhaps I need a new song for *me*, so that I can find a new path to God, an undiscovered territory that is deeper and richer and resonates with a different joy. Perhaps my song is not ended but unfinished. Perhaps if I listen in this silence, I will hear a different melody, so that I can sing a new prayer.

It is all prayer, all grace - every shout, every whisper, every cry of despair. It is all God's music, even the silence. So I will stumble, and pray, and shine light on new pathways, and sing a new song, and find me and God. Ever and again, I will find God. And together, we will sing.

Soft Landing

Somewhere in my first year of sobriety, I went through a rough patch. It may be more accurate to say that "somewhere in my first year of sobriety, I found a few seconds of joy and breathless freedom." Those seconds were very few and very far between. The rough and stumbly, broken and prickly moments stretched into days, into weeks, into months. I (still) feel so much more at home in those spaces. I understand the rules there. There may be more pain in that place, but I get its ebb and flow, understand its motion and oddly circuitous paths.

This time, of all those myriad times, was really pretty rough. Trust me: I know rough.

Now, what they don't tell you, the omnipotent and aloof *They* who haunt the smoky rooms and dingy halls of recovery, what They don't tell you is just how raw, just how naked, just how vulnerable you can feel when you finally start feeling, and there's nothing standing between you and the rest of the world except you.

It's just you. And the pain. And the fear. And the fire that burns inside your head because you just can't stop thinking and you can't stop feeling and the world keeps spinning and you just want to yell "Stop!" or maybe "Wait!" or maybe just hide. Just crawl under the covers and lie in the cool and shadowy dark for a few thousand years, until It's all gone, until you can't even remember what It was to begin with.

I was consumed by that fire. Those flames licked up one side and down the other, dancing along every inch of my skin without cease. Scorched earth policy (or whatever equivalent fits). I held my breath, held it all in, waiting for it to end, for the burning to stop, for the manicky, panicky beating of my heart to quiet. I held myself breathlessly still, hopelessly folded in on myself.

It was right about then that a friend gave me a card. It was not your typical Hallmark card, replete with hearts and flowers and ooey-gooey sentiment. Nor did it highlight wise, sarcastic characters who made pithy little remarks that you thought were amusing and yet couldn't recall thirty-seven seconds later. In fact, this card had a cartoon-like (think Keith Harrington-esque rather than Boynton-y) picture of a big city skyline, a suspension bridge in the foreground, and a sunshine yellow taxi clearly falling (at breakneck speed, I imagine) off the edge of the bridge to the depths of whatever it was below, flames shooting out the taxi's windows, and some person, some stick-figure of a person, waited inside, clearly obeying the laws of gravity and motion, clearly at a loss.

The future did not look bright for the taxi or its rider.

On the inside, to the left, were words. Many, many words. Great gobs of words that told the story of how the taxi, and the person inside of it, came to be flying off that particular bridge at that particular time. Or maybe, the words told the story of the thoughts and feelings of that lone and lonely inhabitant as he (or she) plummeted to some cataclysmic crash. Might have been some spiritual allegory. I don't remember. Frankly, I don't really care.

What I remember was the echo I felt of that figure's resignation and absolute acceptance of the act of free falling in an endless and elegant arc that could only end in - not death; that would be too clean, too neat - but more pain. That certainty that this would not end in a bottom but with a trap door.

That was the left-hand side. The right side held a wish. Bold black letters on a blanket of bright white:

I wish for you a soft landing

And at that exact moment, everything started up again. Until that very instant, everything about me had been held in suspended animation, frozen in some weird *danse macabre*, or a game of statues - nothing moved, nothing changed, except the fire in my head and the freely-falling, bottoming out that I could only watch from 30,000 feet and feel with intimate agony.

A wish. A hope. A prayer that buckled my knees and filled me with breathless wonder. A desperately needed lesson in compassion and love from a friend who knew my heart and cherished my soul (even when I could find only tattered bits (when I bothered to look at all)). She understood that compassion has nothing to do with healing me or changing me. It was not advice or wisdom. Comfort didn't really fit either. I was falling, and nothing she could do would stop the descent.

She didn't watch from a great and safe distance, shielding herself from the certain wreckage I was about to cause. She didn't demand that I stop and pull myself together, nor did she coddle me and feed me the casual niceties so easily said (and so blithely become merely pleasant noise).

All she could do was love me and wish for me a soft landing.

These days, my rough patches are not so rough. What seemed so bleak and attenuated now has softly blurred edges and rounded corners. I don't seem to cut myself on my life too often anymore. My head catches fire with stories and words rather than panic and paralysis. Still, I have my moments, and get caught off guard, not by the rawness and the nakedness, but more by despair or grief. Life changes. God, does life change! Thank God that it does, and me along with it.

But for all that it changes, for all that I have been changed, still, one of the dearest prayers I know remains: I wish for you - for me - for us all - a soft landing. No matter our strength or faith or goodness or grace; for all our mended brokenness and razor-edged faults, we all fall sometimes. We all sit in the back of a taxi, hurtling off the bridge at a million miles an hour, falling into forever.

And as we fall, as we plummet to the surety of a trap door bottom, we can still wish for a soft place to land. And in that landing, that soft and gentle landing, may we find a place to breathe, a spot of rest in the palm of God's hand.

1998

Nothing More than Feelings

I have deleted about a hundred opening statements for this essay to date. That I started it only a few minutes ago will give you some perspective on how freaking difficult I find this particular exercise.

Feelings.

Gah. Blank stare into the middle distance. Slight rise in heart rate (the physical heart, not the lumpy, squishy metaphorical, poetic version that gets all ooey-gooey, that skips a beat, that breaks, that sings, that does all those *feeling* things). No, the elevated heart rate and thin patina of cold sweat come from the slightly panicky sensation that washes over me when I think about feeling. *My* feelings, to be exact. Yours are all well and good, honest, forthright, uncomplicated. Mild. Gentle, even.

Me? I have to remind myself that, although I can feel mostly disconnected and disjointed and off-kilter and sad and lost and broken and a few thousand other things, the miracle is that I can "feel" at all. I went for decades honestly believing that I didn't. Or that my feelings went in a straight line between "fine" and "tired." I spent a few eternities believing that my emotions were so powerful that if I allowed myself to actually feel them, they would, most likely, kill me. They were Leviathan, a maelstrom of churning energy, an endless and infinite whirlpool that would suck me down and swallow me whole. I invested in them all the power and capriciousness of an avenging God, waiting to strike out and smite me.

Talk about shut down! It took me years to admit that "tired" is not an emotion. Then it took me a few more years to figure out that I might actually have to learn how to feel something, anything. As numb as I was, that gaping hole inside - the one that tried to keep God out and trapped me in a tiny universe of one, the one that housed my self-loathing and self-doubt, the one that kept me enraptured with self-destruction and addicted to *More*, that blanketed me with isolation and whispered that I might as well drink, because alcohol at least smudged the lines of pain and left in its wake the slow burn of abject surrender - that hole was leaking my stiff control into the real world and I just couldn't do it anymore. I couldn't even stay numb.

I had had glimpses of real joy, even amidst my pain. I had allowed myself a few moments to hope that it could be - would be - better, and the gods did not come to crush me for my bit of presumption. And so began my quest: to learn how to feel, how to be present and sit comfortably in my own skin. I approached the task like I approach a still pond on a hot summer day: toe outstretched, skimming the surface and testing the waters. I splashed in the shallows for a while, water to my ankles, getting acclimated, getting wet, venturing out a bit farther in fits and starts, depending upon how brave I might be at any given moment.

And so I learned. In fits and starts, I learned. Mostly. I get happy and sad and mad and glad - the basics, so I've discovered. And I get wistful and silly and frustrated and bored and joyful and distracted and a thousand other things. Sometimes singly, sometimes in weird pastiches that cycle a hundred feelings in an instant and leave me breathless. I get to feel all that stuff, every day. I stuck my toe in that dark and murky pool, eyes screwed shut, until I could bear to leap. And I leaped. And I was not devoured. I lived to tell the tale.

So why is it, so many years later, that just when I think my head is above water, that my toes have found something solid upon which to stand, everything seems to have shifted, and that solid ground is nothing more than quicksand, sucking me under? When the hell did this happen?

I swear to God - I am a strong and capable woman. I am successful, frighteningly intelligent, witty as hell. Why do I suddenly feel as if I'm mired in a bog, unable to function? The worst part - I can see myself holding the compass, the road map, clearly marked with *"Here be dragons."* I am holding the damned instruction manual in my hands, dammit. I know I have all the tools, right at my fingertips, and yet I seem so incapable of navigating my way through my life.

I know a lot of things, actually. I know that this, too, shall pass. I know that God is with me always. That my only job, really, is to love my son and help him find his own path. That there's nothing so bad that a drink won't make worse. I know that I have been whole but now feel broken. I know I have been caught, redeemed, loved, and now feel lost. I know I still stutter and stumble and avoid the phrases "I don't know" and "I need help."

I know that the longest journey I've ever had to make is the one from my head to my heart. It seems like an endless journey through a trackless, cold and lonely desert.

I've been here before. In a thousand different iterations, I have stood in this spot, lost and lonely and afraid. And I am tired of this introspection. Tired of this interminable quest to figure out what the hell is going on in my life, how I can feel happy in my life, where is God in my life, on and on, *ad nauseum*. At some point, it becomes self-indulgent, and I come off as a pampered *prima dona* (feel free to protest this point, eloquently (yet vehemently), that nothing could be further from the truth). I am so tired of feeling like a tightly wound spring. I don't know how to change this, so I avoid it and go numb. I disconnect: one more piece of pain that I have to confront, and I just can't do it. Not today. I can only pretend to be brave for so long.

I hate having to admit this. I am too old to dance with these ghosts again, too old for this bout of existential angst and self doubt. I want to do it differently, to fix it, and it feels as if I have slammed into a mountain of glass. I can't find a handhold, my feet slip and slide out from under me, leaving me prostrate and bruised.

But here's the difference: all impotence aside, all quivery, fearful drowning-while-immobile, breathless and clueless and broken, I know one more thing: in the face of everything, *act*.

And so I do. In fits and starts, sometimes with feet dragging, I act; I move. And then, I dive. Dive inward, to find God and grace. Leap upward, light the torch, search for a hand to hold in the darkness. I ask for help to find a soft spot upon which to land. How much more miraculous, more holy can it get? How astounding, that in the space between breaths, I find peace and the world changes. This is all holy space. It is measured in the space between you and me. It's all there, the sacred, the holy, surrounding us, connecting us, keeping us whole. Keeping me whole. If I can just commit, just trust, just forgive, just love, then I would know I was in the presence of God.

Life is not what I expected. Life is. That's the deal. It's bumpy and messy and scary and happy and joyous and annoying and surprising, in infinite variety and subtlety. And most of all: changing. I get to participate in that. I get to do it well, screw it up, find moments of grace. In the midst of pain or doubt or joy, or hope, it is not so dark; I am not so alone, as long as I put one foot in front of the other. I get to find God, every day. I can be made whole, every day. I can be healed, every day. None of this comes naturally. It is still easier, at times, to disconnect than to willingly open up my heart. But, I have known God's grace, and I have felt joy and love, and so I struggle gladly to be human, every day.

God is here, in this place with me, and I - -

Today, I know it.

The Holiness of Broken Things

I am fascinated by the idea of wholeness. I think this is true because I have felt so broken for so long. It is a desire of my heart - to feel whole, to be complete.

When I dance among the ladders with the angels, it is my brokenness that I carry with me. Like Luria's Light, I was whole once, and then shattered into an infinity of pieces. I couldn't possibly find all of those myriad pieces, let alone bring them back together, to the center (my center). No healing, no wholeness. Just brokenness. Forever.

It is no surprise that I live a very fragmented life. There are an infinity of boxes cluttering my head, gathering dust. I stuff my shame and my sins in them, my less-than-ness and my fears. I lock them up tight, with rusty chains and bits of string and hide them in little-used and dusty corridors, where they lie in shadow under the flickering lights. All of them are stacked precariously, haphazardly with seemingly little thought to where they sit.

Trouble is, no matter how well I seal them, and I swear that I do, they leak. They seep and ooze and get all sticky and messy. Even my brokenness is broken.

So it was with no small amount of surprise, sitting in morning services last Shabbat, that I realized that this may no longer be quite so true. My brokenness may not be beyond repair. The dream of wholeness - of completion and connection - they are meant for me. *Even for me.* I sat in that service, surrounded by friends and strangers, sound and light, prayer and benediction, I stood in this holy and sacred moment - and I let go. And in that moment, when I gathered all my brokenness - the moldy boxes and the jagged-edged slivers of glass, and released them all - I was made whole.

And here's the thing, as I write this essay at 36,000 feet: I am not broken. I am whole. And this, I think, is always true. I think. I want to believe this. Just as we are always at the Gates, we are always redeemed - we are always whole. It's all the stuff, all the boxes and frayed rope that we stack and store and carry with us that whispers to us (to me) of brokenness. I carry it with me; it is mine to give back.

For today, for this moment, I choose to put my brokenness aside, to breathe in wholeness and feel complete. For this moment, of lightness and freedom, I will dance in joyous wonder, in the palm of God's hand.

I offer this poem, written as my interpretation for the biblical verses known as *Ki Tisa* (Exodus 30:11–34:35). While I know that there is holiness in broken things - there is also holiness and joy and freedom in wholeness, and for that I am eternally grateful.

The Holiness of Broken Things

I carry my brokenness with me
It is holy -
as holy as my breath,
my heart,
my wholeness.

It is a part of me, these
scattered pieces
of shattered longing
and battered dreams.
My sins.
All of them.
I carry them -
all of them;
All these broken things
that bend me and bow me,
together with my wholeness,
these holy things.
Idols to my shame,
wrapped in gold and
adorned in abandon.
I fed the fires of that sacred forge
with fear and guilt,
and the altars ran slick with salted tears.
I offered -
offer -
the broken pieces as
my sin offering,
for they are holy,
and I carry them with me,
together with my wholeness.

I carry my brokenness with me -
all my sins
and shame
and salted tears,
and I place them
together with my wholeness
on the sacred altars
holy, holy, holy.
They twine together in red and gold flames,
Broken
and Whole
offered together
and returned to me ,
Whole
and Broken -
Holy still,
carried together
until I reach the next altar.

Faith Enough

Over the course of a handful or so of years not too long ago, I managed to lose a little bit of everything: stuff, people, things of inestimable value to me - one thing after the next, again and again. And then yet again. Sometimes the pace of loss was so fast I could barely catch my breath or stop long enough to grieve. Worse were the slow and lingering losses. They were excruciating and exquisite disintegrations of heart and spirit.

With each loss, I would hit bottom. Absolute rock-fucking-bottom. I would lay, crumpled and still, every nerve taut and throbbing, fairly singing with the tension of shame and grief and sadness, until I was numb. Numb, and relieved, that at least I had finally found the bottom.

And every time - every single time I sagged in relieved acceptance of my failure - I would find the trap door.

There is always a next level of low. Always.

This was not the life I had planned on. Not that I had actually made a plan for my life. But still, this wasn't it. What the hell - I was a nice Jewish girl from a nice middle class family, living in a nice little middle class suburb. And while I had taken a twistier path than most to that place, there I was: a nice Jewish girl with a husband and a child and a house and a job, living the American Dream.

And then one day, again without plan, I wasn't.

Damn.

Like sugar in water, I watched it all dissolve. I wanted to yell "Stop!" I wanted to scream "Wait!" I needed time. I needed something - *someone* - to fix it, make it better. All I had was me. And clearly, I was not up to it. *Let me just catch my breath. Let me just rest for a minute. A day. Maybe another. Please. The light is too bright, and it's dark and cool under these covers. Let me just sleep a little longer. Let me just die a little bit more.*

You know what's worse than bottoming out when you're a drunk, killing yourself a bottle (a glass, a sip) at a time? Bottoming out sober. Everything is raw. Everything is screaming: your body, the voices in your head, the people you love. Worse: the people who love you, who just want you to get it together, get better, stop being so fucking sad all the time. *Jeezus, Stacey - enough! Get over it already.* It's been weeks. Months. A year. More. Too long to grieve. Too long to be stuck. There I was, a butterfly pinned to a black velvet board, raw and defenseless and twitching.

They got bored with me, my friends. Hell; I got bored with me. I wanted to curve into myself, disconnect from the pain that seeped into and out of every pore.

I wanted to drink.

Almost two decades sober, almost two decades of learning how live without drinking, learning how to live with God, and I wanted to drink. Funny thing - I knew, absolutely *knew* that I would get, *maybe*, 37 seconds. Thirty-seven seconds of relief, where all the noise would just stop, and I would be able to breathe and my skin would stop crawling and I would disconnect enough to not feel and not be. Thirty-seven seconds. And I was in so much pain, it seemed a worthwhile trade: my life, my pain, for thirty-seven seconds.

And I didn't.

I'd lost my marriage, my house, my credit, several jobs, numerous friends and a beloved brother, and I wanted to drink and I wanted to disappear and I didn't. What the hell?

Oh, yeah: faith.

It sweeps in, peeks around corners, stumbles around blindly, in infinite variety, offering healing and grace. At times, it is cool and resonant, a joyful transcendence that leaps and soars. It is fearless, filled with surety and possibility and hope. It is a glorious and mindful act, all breathless wonder and full beyond measure. It illuminates the darkness. It is intimate as love, brave as love, near as love.

And when I'm in that wonky, spiritually fit place, when life is balanced and I'm not teetering on the edge and unfixably broken, this is the faith that fills me. At these times, in that place, everything fits and flows, endlessly effortless - God's in the heavens, all's right with the world. Amen, amen.

This was *not* one of those spiritually wonky places. This wasn't effortless and clean. It was dark and twisty and alone. This was a dangerous and elusive faith, limned in pain, dancing on a razor's edge of hope. This was not a host of angels singing loud hosannas while dancing on the head of a pin. It was a much more difficult faith, like pebbles strewn across an impossibly huge plain. Almost insurmountable. Almost invisible. Almost.

But in all these impossible almosts, there was God. In the midst of the jagged edges of my pain (no less so than in the midst of that impossibly joyous and majestic sweep of calming grace), there was God.

So what does that get me? What good is God, or faith, when it is broken despair that is transcendent, driving me? Where was God? And why? Why God, and faith, when we are still stripped and laid bare, when the only prayer we can offer is "Screw you, God?" What the hell does faith get us, when the money is running out and the solitude swallows you whole and the road shifts suddenly, bedrock becoming quicksand in the space between breaths?

What good is faith? Even then - especially then: there is faith, and God. Faith does not mean that I will never know pain again, or fear. People will die, foreclosures will happen, jobs will be lost. Of course, miracles will happen, too, along with acts of breathtaking kindness and astounding courage. *Life* will happen, in all its messy glory. And faith, sometimes a grand, sweeping gesture, sometimes blind and leaping - faith allows me to put one foot in front of the other. No matter how small the step, no matter how faltering, I put one foot in front of the other, and know that I will be carried through.

And with that act of faith and defiance - that has everything to do with love and hope and grace and God - life changes. The world changes. *I* am changed. Changed enough to put one foot in front of the other, again. And that, I am sure, is faith enough.

Hope Stronger than Fear

Brokenness, Wholeness and Sobriety

For all the blessings that fill me, for God's grace that lifts me, for all who teach me, simply, to live a sober life and hear God's voice, I give thanks, with humble and profound gratitude.

*I sent my hope out into
the Universe.
Whispered and weightless,
and waited
For hope
to lift me,
to fill me,
to save me,
to heal me.
and so be Holy
once more.*

Anger stops us from choosing happiness.

The Music of God (Part 1)

When I was born - or something near enough to that so that it doesn't matter - I sang. I can't remember a time I didn't sing. Spiders. Buses. Bonnie Over the Ocean harmonized with Christmas carols and *Hinei Mah Tov*. I drank it in and sang it out - every note, every key, every word.

Even then, I knew that when I sang, I was free. Or freed. Something. I felt light and joy, and I loved how people would stop when I sang, and watch me, in wonder or something close to happiness. And when I was finished, when the song was done, invariably, they would coo and smile and tell me how beautifully I sang.

And in that exact moment, I knew that I was beautiful. I knew that I was loved. Just for that instant, even as my face grew pink and warm, and my toes curled at their compliments, and I felt like squirming under their attention, in that instant I knew that I could sing and it was good.

I don't remember a time I didn't sing. From first grade junior choir at synagogue to the middle school chorus and my high school stage (with summer theater camp weaving all in and through those years), name a musical and I was probably in it. Name a song arranged in four part choral harmony, and I sang it: first soprano, reaching flawlessly all the way up to F above high C. And oh - it was all amazingly good! For the space of that performance, and the handful or two of minutes while the applause lasted and the congratulations echoed off the auditorium walls, it was good and I was loved and God was near.

And when I was 18 or 20 or some other difficult and existentially angsty age, I decided I would never sing again. There were a thousand reasons for my declaration, every one of them reasonable, well thought out.

They were all lies, of course.

I didn't sing - *refused* to sing - because I was angry - with the world, my life, my family. And God. Oh, I was especially angry with God! And what I wasn't angry with, I was afraid of - everybody, everything. Singing was the one thing - the only thing - that allowed me to step outside my own head and breathe, really breathe, and feel the presence and comfort and absoluteness of God. In a world where the ground was constantly shifting, where people loved you and told you lies, where less-than and lost were my constant companions, there was God. And one day, at some impossibly vulnerable, hormonal age, I crawled outside the confines of my head, and was met with emptiness.

Where once there was God, now was a howling, empty loneliness, coupled with the absolute conviction that I was alone and God had gone. Somewhere. Anywhere. Certainly gone from *me*. I thrummed like a taut wire: abandoned by God and fairly buzzing with tension in the face of my inability to fit inside my own skin or into the steady cadence of life the rest of the world seemed to find so easily.

I tried. I tried to find God, to fill that gaping open space. For a bunch of years, I searched, but eventually, I couldn't bear the thought of my abandonment. A few years into that howling emptiness, so vulnerable and so desperately raw, my twisted logic led me to the only possible conclusion that made sense: having been rejected by God, I therefore rejected the one thing that felt like holiness, the one thing that lifted me to sacred. I'll show *You*, I declared into the silence that suddenly filled me: *I will not sing*. Instead, it was so much easier, so much more right, to crawl inside a bottle and hide there for a small space of eternity and my own personalized tour of hell. It seemed like the right thing to do at the time.

So, for the next couple of decades, I didn't. And I did.

For the next couple of decades, I did not sing. For the next couple of decades, I hid inside a bottle of whatever was handy, as long as it burned like liquid oblivion going down, and made me believe, if even for 37 seconds, that I was not alone in the universe, and the voices in my head stopped whispering their siren song of self-destruction.

For the next couple of decades, I yearned for the connection I had once found in singing. And for the next couple of decades, I denied myself the grace of it, with ever sip, every glass, every hangover. There was *a lot* of denial.

For more than twenty years, I did not sing. And then I got sober.

I got sober, and they told me, all those happy, shiny people who filled the smoky rooms and the cracked leather couches and the gunmetal folding chairs that had seen better decades, let alone better days - they told me to find God.

I didn't need to *find* God. Hell, I knew exactly where I'd left Him. Her. "The Deity." I hate the grammar of the Divine. God was locked away in a private little room, *watching*. Watching everything through a window that looked out onto the world far, infinitesimally far away. God's face was the face of Compassion itself - filled with kindness and mercy and love. And God wept, as He watched, at the evil and cruelty and waste and sadness that filled the earth, day in and day out, world without end, amen.

God wept, and I saw that Her hands were bound with barbed wire, powerless to act, impotent in the face of a desperately broken world and desperately broken people. What good was God, if God could only watch, and weep?

I may have known (unequivocally) exactly where God was hiding, but I searched anyway. They told me to, those happy, shiny, sober people. And they had something I didn't have, something I desperately wanted: they had joy. They had happy. They sat comfortably in their own skins, didn't seem to want to crawl out of it all the time, into a hole or the dark or... away. And I wanted that. All of it. I wanted to be made whole, to fit, to be forgiven. So if the price of all that was to seek God - seek God I would, in twelve step meetings and self help books, spiritual guides and therapy. I would practice willingness, because they said it was the next right thing to do.

I managed to make a friend at a meeting; turns out we had more than trying to stay sober a day at a time in common. He was edgy, sarcastic, broken, looking for redemption and God, and he was Jewish. My lucky day. He tended to go temple-hopping on Saturday mornings and invited me to hop along. Not every Saturday, but every so often, I'd hop along with him, and look for God in God's own house.

I stumbled through the prayers. I didn't remember the choreography or the Hebrew. I was convinced that I didn't fit, didn't belong. I didn't know what the hell I was doing, and felt gauche and ungainly. I had that odd and unsettling, questioning, searching, just-at-the-tip-of-my-out-of-reach -almost-discovery -of-I-wish-I-knew-or-maybe-I-hope-I-don't-discover   sensation   of being *closerthanthis* to an answer kind of thing. But it was elusive and missing, an almost-whisper of grace.

And then one Saturday morning, the choir sang.

From above me and behind me, a host (I swear it was a host, not just a handful or two of earnest choristers) a *host* of heavenly voices filled the sanctuary with this glorious, transcendent sound, a rising arc of prayer and joy.

It was rich and full and resonant. I could hear in it, in every note, every chord that stretched from one note into a thousand (I *swear* it was a thousand) before tumbling back - like water, or laughter - into a single note again, and there was God: unshackled, unbound, present in a way that took my breath away.

And I knew - *knew* - that everyone around me felt it. They got it - they were in it and of it and surrounded by it. They were whole and filled and it was all meant for them. This was the day that God had made, and they were welcomed into the miracle of that moment. I could feel their faith, their acceptance - of God, of themselves, of the world around them - radiating outwards, a parallel arc to this music of God.

I stood transfixed. I felt the power of that faith, the grace and majesty of it. I wanted it, every drop, every heartbeat, every breath. I could feel the hunger in me build, a surge of want and need. I stood at the jumping off place, poised and motionless at the gate. A step. All I needed was a single step *through,* and I would find it, all of it, all my yearning answered - faith, redemption, forgiveness. God.

And I couldn't. I couldn't step or leap or even move. I could only stand, rooted, outside of that glorious, joyous song, knowing that there was faith and forgiveness and God. For them - all of them, the world entire. But not for me.

I stood, and I wept, and I did not sing, knowing that my fear was stronger than any faith, louder than any music, vaster and more complete than God.

I was silent, and I knew that my silence would last forever.

The Music of God (Part 2)

Here's a curious thing: the English words "miracle" and "mirror" come from the same Latin root: *mirari*, which means "to wonder at." It is meant to convey a sense of awe and amazement.

Funny. I read this in a fantasy novel a thousand years ago (Ok, maybe not a thousand. Maybe it was closer to 35 or 40. But you know, as big as "a thousand" sounds, I gotta tell you - at the age of old-plus-two, "35 or 40 years ago" sounds positively ancient). It was Peter S Beagle's *The Last Unicorn*. In it, Schmendrick the Magician (and how could you not absolutely adore a magician named Schmendrick?), tells another character (a Unicorn masked as a human woman), who is searching desperately - and then less so desperately as time stretches out for far too long (though maybe it was just long enough) - for others of her kind) (Unicorns, that is, not humans, or even unicorns masked as humans).

Anyway, the now-human unicorn, writing a letter to the King or some other power-that-was, in order to make a request asks the Magician how to spell "miracle," (because she was looking for one right about then) and Schmendrick replies (I paraphrase) "Miracle is spelled with two Rs, since it comes from the same root as "mirror." Schmendrick then proceeds to blithely muck up his magic and spells for almost the rest of the book, until the very end, when he stops trying quite so hard to do it right, and just *hopes* that it will all work out in the end.

Spoiler alert: it does. Sort of. I guess hoping is a kind of wild magic all its own.

I remember, all those long and dusty years ago, because it really is a marvelous and poignant story, I remember thinking "Wow. I love that! What an awesome thought, totally fraught with meaning. I have no idea what the meaning is, but I am absolutely certain that it's huge." (Again, I paraphrase)

As with Schmendrick, I then proceeded to blithely muck up my life something fierce, until the very end. Well, not the end of my life, but certainly, for years and years and countless years of pain and pity and fear, of brokenness and isolation and silence - until the very bitter edges of that life. I was a mess, and my life was worse.

And then I got sober.

I seem to use that plot device more often than not. I say that, somewhat tongue in cheek, but really; it was a death-defying moment, getting sober. It was a watershed, the parting of the seas of my addiction to More, my almost lifelong love affair with self destruction. It was an instantaneous and painfully attenuated moment: from one second to the next, in the blink of an eye, the beat of my heart - on one side, the certainty of death and madness. On the other, a path. A chance. Freedom.

Hope (that is a wild magic all its own, even for me).

Ah, sobriety.

Ugh.

I do not know how I survived those early days (months) (ok, years). Being a drunk was easy by comparison. I was infinitely (intimately) more comfortable with my well-lubricated life. I craved separation: anything to put some distance between me and my tormentors. So what if the tormentors were me? I blamed you for my isolation, anyway. And I blamed God for my pain.

Suddenly, life went from slippery and slick to raw and naked and much more present than I ever imagined or wanted. I swear, there were days (hours) (minutes even) that I felt as if I were caught in a steel and sharp-toothed trap, and if I could have gnawed away some phantom limb to escape it, I would have.

Suddenly, I went from having no people in my life to having too many, all of them shiny, happy, cheerful people who liked to hug and laugh and speak in niceties until I wanted to scream. But I couldn't get enough of them. I craved their company and dreaded the idea of going home, to my apartment filled with its ghosts and its silence.

Suddenly, I went from no God (or at least a distantly absent One) to a very present God. I knew, without a doubt, that I had a God in my life, and I knew, without a doubt, that my God was God's evil twin brother, out to screw with me, trip me up and make me sweat.

Maimonides argued that God could only be defined in the negative. To do otherwise would limit the might and power and limitlessness of God. I learned, slowly - and not without my own pain and drama - I learned to define God in hindsight.

I learned to find God behind me, in my past. I called these the God Moments. You might call them coincidences or random chance. Happenstance, perhaps, if you were trying to impress. I'm okay with any of that. I am not very particular in what name you or I may use to call God. Much more important for me, in my infinitely grateful hindsight, is that I *call out* - in anger (and, oh, I was filled with anger, there at the end and for the long stretch of my beginning) or joy, pain or doubt or sorrow or wonder. Anything and everything.

And I did. I learned, in fits and starts, I learned to call. To trust.

But there was still no music in it (certainly none that I could hear) (and certainly none that I would let you hear). For all that I was learning to find God again, I would do it without the one way that ever made sense, that ever worked, that ever connected me to whatever name for God you may want to use.

I would not sing.

When I get very quiet, when I get very honest, I will grudgingly admit that, in actuality, I was afraid to sing. Afraid of my voice and what it would sound like after years and years of disuse (not to mention the years and years of abuse). Afraid that even when I sang again, if I ever did, I would no longer be able to find God, no longer be able to dance that holy path up and out, in joy and reverence and grace. I was terrified that I would be trapped in my silence forever.

God, but it was noisy in my head without any music - noisy and jangly and dissonant. Fear is like that - sharp-edged and soulless, a chaos of silence.

And then, somewhere in there, somewhere in all that silence and fear, I took my son to Sunday school for the first time. He was six. I hadn't set foot in a synagogue in years. I hadn't had a formal conversation with God in just shy of forever - so long that I wouldn't have known what to say if I felt the need (desire) (want) to say anything at all.

But Nate was six, and it was time. I knew no one, picked the synagogue out of a hat (or the pixelated internet version of a hat), and walked him into a brick-and-mortar building at the end of a long and lonely road. I walked into this structure and heard the strum of an A-minor chord being played, and I was freed.

Just like that. Freed. If not instantaneously, pretty close to it. I stood in that brick-and-mortar building and suddenly it was a holy place. That one chord, that melancholy, joyous, yearning chord found me, found my silence, and unlocked the chains I had so carefully set in place, to bind me to my fear.

The music of my soul, the song of my heart: yearning. It is neither want nor need, though they are certainly present in it. The song I hear is more a reaching up, a reaching out - in hope, in joy, in despair and desolation. It is a flame that flickers and leaps upward, dancing and guttering and glowing through it all. It's an A-minor, sweet and knowing and raw. It's a question, a prayer, a fluid and graceful arc that moves in you and through you. It's the heart's cry in the darkness "Where are You?" and the breathless hope of God's answer "*Hineini* - here I am."

Hope is its own wild magic, its own sacred benediction.

With that one chord, I found my voice again, left the silence behind. It was the voice of my desire, and in it, I found blessing and grace. In it, I found miracle and mirror both, wonder and awe and hope. And when I opened up again, finally, when I lifted my voice in song again, when I finally believed that my hope was stronger than my fear, I found my song, and myself again.

And in that song, there was God.

Hineini.

Hope Enough to Share

I have a friend who is going through some big and scary stuff: life-altering, soul-changing, potentially transformative and possibly transcendent stuff. "I don't know what to do. I don't know what will happen. I feel so alone," she said. Her pain was palpable.

God, I know that place - that sticky, scary, prickly place. Crossroads? I wish it were as simple as that! That place isn't a fork in the road; it's a whole damned service for twelve, all jumbled and junk-drawer worthy, a snake pit of messy choice. It isn't dark. Dark implies the possibility of something not-dark. This is the total absence of light. It is a teetering precipice, the pain of the present licking at your feet, coiling upwards, while the fear of the unknown breathes hot and harsh on your skin and presses you down,

This place is **alone**.

My friend's words take me back to my early days in recovery. I spent hours in those meeting rooms, on beat-up couches, drinking horrible coffee, breathing in air that reeked of cigarette smoke and bleach and stale sweat. Hours upon hours of shiny happy people and their endless chatter, who had miraculously been plucked from the depths of their despair and given new life. New hope. And they passed it on to me. Headier than any wine, more intoxicating than any drink I'd ever guzzled. Hope. In the telling of their stories, I found hope.

"I've been there," they all said, in some iteration or other.

No fanfare, no drama. Just this quiet moment of intimate connection. They'd *all* been there — that same place where I had stood, rooted and lost and broken and alone. It may have looked different from the outside– some talked of boardrooms on Wall Street, others of a gutter in the slums – those exteriors were facades that hid our utter devastation from public view. How could I not find healing in these words? How could I not take hope? They sat pretty comfortably in their own skins, putting one foot in front of the other. Moving, acting, choosing, deciding. Feeling. Feeling *everything*. Not drinking. *Not drinking.* And they shared that all, with me, with each other, every day, endlessly, hour after hour. It got so I believed I could do all that too.

And after the hours and hours of bad coffee and stale smoke and endless, hopeful chatter, they left. And I went home. Alone. Home, to an empty apartment that echoed. Home, to sit and think and climb the walls, to feel the silence pound. While I didn't crawl into a bottle, I climbed into my head, taking refuge in that nightmare landscape of my own creation, with this chorus singing hollowly, keeping me company: *In the end I stand here alone. For all their laughter and sharing and connection, I come home alone. And who will be there to catch me when I fall, when I fail?*

I don't know what to do. I don't know what will happen. I feel so alone.

That place. *That* fear. That place that is absent of light. I know this place all too well.

In the end, we are all of us alone. But here's the miracle, that bit of grace within that singular moment of clarity: there are breadcrumbs. Strewn along that rocky, tortuous, treacherous path, with all its traps and quicksand and trails that go nowhere and the scary monsters who hide behind the poison-spitting trees, there are breadcrumbs. There are stories and connections and hope, left for us by those who've gone before. And if we're lucky — really, really lucky — there are hands to hold in the darkness, torches placed along the way.

Yes, I take my leaps alone. Yes, even now, I can stand rooted in the muddy, messy Middle, unable to go back, afraid to move forward. But there is hope. Grace. Hands to hold, torches that shine. And should I fail, should I fall, I will be caught. God, or some Higher Power whose name I don't yet know will allow me rest and comfort until I'm ready to go it again.

I'm here, I tell my friend. *Feel free to fly, to fall. To hope. I've been there my friend. I'll be waiting for you, breadcrumbs in hand, and hope enough to share.*

Boxing with God

I have a couple issues with God.

Anyone who's known me longer than, say, five minutes, can pretty much figure that out. I wanted to change my relationship status on Facebook to show that I'm in a relationship with God and "it's complicated." I have run the gamut from at-one-with-the-All, sitting in virtual lotus on top of my virtual mountain, at peace and in love with God and all of God's wondrous works, to being convinced that *my* Higher Power is God's evil twin brother, whose sole Divine Purpose is to mess with me and my life. I struggle with God's blessings and God's capriciousness.

My journey with God has been rocky at best. At thirteen, I announced my intention to become a rabbi. This had less to do with a belief in God and more to do with being a Jew. As I saw it then, if I had to take God along with being a good Jewish rabbi, so be it. As my parents saw it, this was *not* a good career move for a nice Jewish girl. They were quite sure that I would never make enough money as a rabbi to keep me living in the style to which they would have liked for me to become accustomed. They laughed, I caved, but maintained my love for Judaism (and by extension, God).

By fifteen, I declared my apostasy: God was a lie. Or dead. Or an opiate of the bourgeoisie masses. Take your pick. It was two weeks before confirmation, and I was a teenager, filled with anger and fueled by existential angst. Simmering with contempt, I announced that I no longer believed in God and that to become confirmed would be hypocritical. I refused to participate (and did a secret little happy dance of joy to see the light dim just a little bit in the eyes of my parents).

And so, although I did not know it then, began The Great Quest. I had a God-sized hole in the middle of me, and it ached to be filled. I filled it with anything handy. Sarcasm. Contempt. Cynicism. As I got older, there were other drugs. Sex. Intellectualism. Throw them all in there - anything that would make me not feel quite so empty, quite so lost. Anger was good. If I stayed angry enough, pointed enough fingers, sneered with just the right curl of the lip, I did not have to feel. Anger was almost enough to fill in the empty spaces, almost enough to wrap around me like a shield, protect me from my fear. After anger came alcohol. Emergency spirituality in liquid form. I loved drinking. I loved feeling that wet fire trail down my throat and nestle in my stomach. I loved the way it made my fingertips buzz, an electric pulse that made me want to dance and move and breathe. The noise in my head got quiet and I could think. I could float, bathed in that clear, clean sharp liquid that made me feel beautiful and connected and almost (but not quite) human.

Anger and alcohol - my constant companions for years. They kept my demons at bay. They blurred the outlines of that god-sized hole, and if I stayed angry enough, drank enough, I could almost believe that they filled that hole, filled *me*. I could tell myself that they were enough, and that I was enough. And that tiny little whisper that skittered and skipped in the dark corners of my head? The one that never quite believed those lies that I told myself, those lies I so desperately wanted to believe? Those whispers were all but drowned out by the crushing tide of my drinking.

And then I got sober, for a whole host of reasons, not least of which was the fact that the anger and the alcohol stopped working. I couldn't get to that floaty, breathy place anymore. Couldn't find God, or at least what I thought passed for God. Couldn't find any quiet space. All that was left was this deafening white noise and a brittle coating of despair.

So I got sober, and all those shiny happy people sitting in those shiny happy rooms of recovery, where the smoke hung in grey-blue wisps and the coffee could peel paint (unless it was more just brownish warmed water with a hint of caffeine) and the smell of ammonia masked the stale sweat and salted tears and the free floating anxiety that bordered on fear of the masses of people who laughed and cried and wondered and wandered and quested and questioned - all those people insisted that I find a God.

Great. Give me a task that I have been failing at for decades. I'll get right on that (where the hell is the sarcasm font when you need it?!)

And strangely enough, I *did* get right on that. I started my quest for God in earnest. I had my eyes peeled for The Answer, that sublimely written piece of prose that would explain away all my doubt, all my cynicism, all my uncertainty, leaving me glowing with the light of God and giving me comfort and relief and calm. And I looked, and I read, and I looked some more. I sweated and struggled and stamped my foot. And everything I read confirmed my belief that God was a little hinky. Or maybe the wrong religion. Certainly capricious and inconsistent. God was messy and vindictive and totally missing.

And the more I looked, the more I struggled, the more desperate I became to find that source of solace. I saw my friends get it. I saw them, sitting comfortably in their own skins, whole (for the most part), healing (for the most part). Recovering (for the most part). And I wasn't getting it. I was just as far away from God as when I was fifteen. God may be real for everyone else - and I was genuinely happy for all those people, really; but God would never be real for me.

I remember one Saturday, going to synagogue with one of my friends. I figured that as long as I was supposed to look for God, I may as well look inside God's house. As I sat in the sanctuary, soothed by the beauty of the stained glass, uplifted by its cathedral ceilings, comforted by the familiar heft of the prayer book, I listened to the choir as it sang out some hymn of praise, some psalm offered up to God. And I wept. I was so close! I could hear their joy; I could! I wanted to reach out and grab it, hold onto it, *connect* with it. They were all so *sure*. They rested in the palm of God's hands, carried across the chaos of their doubts, the noise and tumult of the universe. They *got* it, all of it. And as much as I knew that, I knew that I never would get that gift. I knew that I would forever be denied that peace. How could I not weep in the face of that?

I told myself it didn't matter really. Told myself I didn't care, and that God and redemption and grace were fine for other people, but really, I certainly didn't need them. I was doing just fine, thank you. So what if I was a little raw, felt a little exposed? So what if I had created an invisible hard candy coating that kept me safe and separate and disconnected? So what if despair coiled around my ankles and drifted upwards, soft and smooth as lies, threatening to choke me? So what if all I wanted to do was drink?

So I planned it. I couldn't take it anymore. I couldn't sleep anymore. Stopped going to meetings, mostly. Couldn't bear to listen to those shiny happy people who had found God - my God, their God, a God: some higher power who carried them and loved them and healed them and redeemed them. I needed to drown out the little voice in my head that insisted, in its silken and seductive and smoky voice, the one that said that I had not rejected God so many years before, but that God had rejected me, and the only thing powerful enough to drown it out, keep God out, was a drink.

There I sat: Queen of the Dramatic Gesture, in my darkened living room, candles flickering and casting macabre shadows on the walls, a cat tangling between my feet, my heart sounding a loud tattoo of determination and fear and wistfulness. I sat in the darkness, planning to drink. I wanted it. Wanted the sweet burn and liquid fire. Wanted the thirty-seven seconds (at best) of absolute release that alcohol gave me. My fingers curled around the neck of that bottle, the glass cool against my palm, calm acceptance settling over me.

And I sank to my knees. I had every intention of drinking. I could taste it, for God's sake! I wanted it, wanted the release and the blankness and the tingle. And yet I sank to my knees. And I cried out from the sere desert of my soul "I give. I can't do this anymore. I can't be so alone. Please help."

That was my prayer. The only prayer I could offer. And I sat on my knees, hands still cradling that damned bottle, and I didn't drink. There were no angels to dance on the head of a pin. There was no clap of thunder or heavenly choir to sing out "Hosanna!" But I did not drink. I did not drink, even though I wanted to, even though every fiber of my being ached to drink. I did not. And I slept - the whole night through. For the first time in months, I slept, not like a baby (up every two hours, hungering for something, cranky and whiny), but like the dead - deep and uninterrupted.

Redemption. I have no doubt that I was offered this glorious gift, along with a small touch of grace. And in that instant, with no angels dancing, no thunderous chorus, I lay down my struggle with God, for God, found God. I was redeemed, at last. The miracle was for me, at last. And I slept.

And now, it's more than a decade later. Through the grace of God, I have still not taken that drink. I have found a faith that gives me comfort, that carries me through those long dark nights of the soul.

I still have them. Still tend to box with God and demand that God be accountable for divine (in)action, just as God demands that I be accountable for mine. We are locked in an eternal embrace, God and me - a lover's embrace, intimate, profoundly connected, bound together as blithely as light, as strong as love. I struggle with the idea of God still. I struggle still with God; after all, I am a true Daughter of Israel. Sometimes it is daily, sometimes not. I rail at God and demand to be comforted, to be carried, to be loved. To be enough (for me, for God). And I am still given grace, because I know that when I ask, I am redeemed. When I love, I am enough. And, wrapped in that blanket of grace, I sleep.

God of the Ocean

There was a time that I doubted the existence of God.

To be totally honest, it was less that I didn't believe in God and more that I wasn't quite sure that God believed in me. I wanted the God of Infinite Compassion. What I got instead was God's Evil Twin Brother. While I had little evidence of God's mercy and love as it played out in my life, I had ample evidence of how God (or His Evil Twin) was really trying to screw with me. I knew, from an early age, that I was lost and alone, slightly broken and beyond repair. It was all God's fault.

It was so much easier to deny God than to face the idea that I had been abandoned. So much easier to defy God than hunger for a redemption that never came.

And I defied God with a vengeance. I thumbed my nose at Him, ignored Her, talked trash whenever I could. Talked loudly, and with passion. I wanted to hurt God, just as I had been hurt. I vowed to never sing again - the one thing I had that brought me a sense of peace and wholeness, the one thing that led me on a shining and sure path to God and grace. I gave that up in a heartbeat. It seemed like a good idea at the time. I drank too much, to drown out the silence of God. If not alcohol, anything: drugs, shopping, food or sex. I used everything I could to bolster my doubt, to delight in my heresy.

That'll teach Him. Ha.

I spun through my life like a whirling dervish. It was a mad dance, and I careened off people and places with equal vigor and disregard. I reveled in my movement, ratcheted up the speed. I was a ghost in my own life, untouched and disconnected. Empty.

I carried that little pocket of emptiness with me everywhere. It was familiar, like a worn old robe that slips on so easily, that drapes just right against the contours of your body - covering, concealing, comforting. I could forget about my war with God and belief and just move faster into the empty, all sensation, devoid of meaning. One night, one day, again and again, stretching into eternity, pure and empty. And it was good.

I drank my way, stumbling and frenetic, with brief forays into over-indulgence of every kind, to California. Fueled by the passion of social justice, I flirted with the belief that if I acted with integrity, that integrity would transfer to me, by osmosis or proximity or luck. I would feel unbroken at last. I hungered for wholeness, drowned it with alcohol, prayed to a God I was convinced was an illusion, who could not hear and who would refuse me at every turn.

And then I stood in the ocean.

We had taken an Adventure Day, we rabble-rousers, we agitated agitators. We took a day off from saving the world and drove down the coast from San Francisco to Santa Cruz, to play and cavort and drink. We basked in the sun, let the salt breeze caress our pale skin, wandered the boardwalk without thought or care. We laughed easily, and teased mercilessly. We were released at last from the social and political battles that had defined us and given us purpose for so long. We devoured the day and wandered into the mist of evening almost spent.

We ended where the earth ends, where earth and mist and water come together in ceaseless susurration and motion. No one had ever told me, this Midwestern child, how noisy the ocean could be. No one had told me how the ocean could excite every one of my senses, make them tingle and feel alive as if for the first time.

I wandered away from my friends, drawn to the edge of the sea. I stood there, the water lapping against my ankles, licking up my calves, the salt drenching my skin and tangling in my hair, the moon - huge and round, the golden light skipping along the waves in a path to eternity - the moon rising like a promise, surrounded by the laughing roar of water and sky. I stood there, amid the vast and endless sea, in the gathering night, and met God, at last.

My God: the God of Infinite Compassion, of light and sound and forgiveness. God of the Ocean.

It was all so huge, so boundless. No one had ever told me. No one told me that, in the face of all that holiness, the truest prayer is not spoken but heard. And for the first time, I listened. I quieted and calmed my heart and my fear, and I listened my prayer, a whisper of moonlight and a shout of the tide. I was so very small against that moon-kissed horizon, and I felt comfort and peace and whole.

I listened, and my prayer was forgiveness, my prayer was redemption. My prayer was love. I stood motionless, exhausted and enthralled. Empty still, but ready to be filled. Broken still, but ready to be healed. I listened a prayer again, and at last, there was love, and God.

Epiphany at the Gas Station

'Tis the season, I guess, to talk of epiphanies. I am in need of one. Of course, when I talk of epiphanies, I always think in terms of angels dancing on the head of a pin, thunder and lightning, heavenly hosts singing hosanna to the Most High. I want the drama, the wonders and portents. I crave drama. It feels more real, for some inexplicable reason, when I am snatched back from the very brink of despair and dire straits.

I want the earthquake, God as a Pillar of Fire. What I mostly get is the still small voice.

Apparently, I get what I need. Apparently, what I needed was the quiet voice of a stranger to give me that moment of clarity that allows me to hear the voice of God.

This was years ago. Couple of decades at best guess. I was breaking into Corporate America through a side door. Having worked for a national poor people's organization for several years, whose unspoken guiding principle seemed to be "to organize the poor you have to be poor," and not being a trust fund baby like so many of my long-term colleagues, I was ready to actually explore the borders of capitalism in all its glory. Don't get me wrong: I wasn't interested in becoming a capitalist. No, I wanted to exploit the system for all it was worth.

I was approaching thirty, and everything I owned fit in the trunk of my car. I had moved back and forth across the country about fifteen times in four or five years. It got to be that I knew, anytime I bought something that wouldn't quite fit in my car, my boss would fly into town and tell me where the next adventure would be. It was never around the corner. Mostly, it involved uprooting my rather tenuous life and driving several hundred miles, fueled by caffeine and the fervent, clear-eyed zeal of the True Believer in social justice.

After years of this nomadic existence, I was finally back in Chicago. It was winter. It was cold. Really, really cold. After a few months, the fateful phone call. Not even a visit this time: time to pack up again, this time for the balmy climes of Minneapolis. In January. I couldn't do it. Just couldn't start over one more time. I was tired. I was done. I quit. Now what?

Seriously: now what? What could I possibly do, career-wise? I had a degree in history and experience rousing the rabble, as it were. What the hell was I going to do with the rest of my life? Honestly, the prospect of living on my parents' floor did not fill me with whelm. I remember reading a want ad for the CIA. They were looking for spies, wanted someone smart, who spoke two or more languages and offered good benefits, including on-site daycare. Talk about early indoctrination! Sadly, I fit the bill. Instead of leaping at my chance to dabble in covert affairs, I drifted towards something else equally suspect in my mind, and sidled into the halls of Corporate America through the time-honored tradition of nepotism. My brother had a gig and gave me a job. From community organizer to insurance salesperson in one easy step. I held my nose and jumped, trying hard not to look back.

Trouble was, my life didn't change quite as much as I thought it would. I was still broke - or so close to broke that it made no real difference. My adherence to Democratic Socialism still rested firmly on the shoulders of my father's very capitalistic law practice (as my parents were so quick to point out). My wardrobe still consisted mainly of loose, comfortable black, although every so often, I threw in a belt to give my clothes some shape. I still slept on the floor of my parents' home. Everything I owned still fit in the trunk of my car.

My car.

My car was becoming quite the issue. It was old and tired. My knowledge of all things auto was severely lacking. I knew to put gas in it. I was vaguely aware that oil was involved in some way. Even with my singular lack of expertise, I knew something was amiss. The car was complaining to me, softly at first, then with increasing stridency: grinding and squeaking, all the while hesitating a bit, chugging a bit more, begging for rest and respite in its car-like, pitiful way. With every passing day, I could feel it poised for total failure. Tires. Exhaust. Heating. Cooling. I'm sure that Newton's Laws of Motion were in question in regards to my car, especially as they relate to acceleration, which my car did only after I said please and thank you and left small gifts and other automotive sacrifices on the hood. The problems loomed large.

And me? I just kept driving, eyes straight ahead, all willful defiance and determined nonchalance. If I refused to acknowledge impending doom, I reasoned, then there could, by definition, be no doom. That I took my life in my hands (and, by extension, the rest of the driving public) every time I got behind the wheel was something that entered my mind only when it got very, very quiet. Since my method of car repair involved intensive use of the volume control knob on my radio, quiet was never a reality. Loud goes a long way in all things repair. If you don't hear the grinding, squeaking, gasping, rattling, coughing knocks and noises, then they don't exist. Right?

This state of plausible deniability went on for months. With every new noise, every new stutter, every desperate twist of the volume knob, my shoulders hunched just a bit more, my breathing strained and got more shallow. Everything wrong with the car got all tangled and twisted and enmeshed. It was fast becoming like that giant ball of string that gets lost in the junk drawer: no beginning, no end, no real hope to unravel it. I was broke. I was lost. I was facing a solid, impenetrable wall of Broken, all-encompassing and infinite in its looming menace, and had no resources to face it or fix it. Like Atlas, I carried this weight on my shoulders, and all I wanted to do was shrug. And me, being me, just piled on each new problem more precariously, higher and higher, until the pile threatened to topple and bury me under its weight.

Months into this insane dance, I stopped at a gas station. Gas I could handle. Mostly. While I was there, filling my tank, one of the mechanics came out. "One of your headlights is out," he said, nodding at the offending lamp.

I laughed, and I think some of my bitterness slipped just a bit. "One more piece of Broken," I said.

And that's when it happened. That's when the guy transformed (transcended? ascended? transmogrified?) from mechanic to avatar of God. Or at least God's messenger. Or something equally holy. I sat in my car, that shivering, sputtering lump of metal, held together with nothing more than hope, and the waters of all that was broken and heavy parted, separated before me, to show a clear, dry, smooth path to the other side.

The mechanic/avatar/messenger said: "You know, we could run a diagnostic on the car, figure out everything that's wrong, and then fix them one by one."

One by one? Wait. What?

My brain spluttered at the thought: one by one? Nonononono, I shouted loudly into my silent internal landscape. It is a lonely and wind-torn place, a black hole of forever where I go and set up camp, hunkering down for the long dark nights of my soul. It's a bad neighborhood and I wander its tumbledown streets alone with some regularity, mugging myself and my psyche every so often. My car is a giant ball of tangled messy string, a mobius strip of problems, an eternal quagmire of broken, with no beginning and no end.

And not just my car (though how simple if that were the case). I ran my life like this: collected stray bits of problems and hurts and slights and sadnesses and fears and doubts and rolled them all into a ball and hid them all away, ashamed and overwhelmed and convinced that if I ignored them all long enough, they would just all melt away, leaving me whole and pure and happy once again. There was so much, and they all just festered and rotted and melted together until they became one, a leviathan of Bad, immense and hungry and devouring.

And here, unasked for, was grace: get it all down and act, one by one.

I cannot do forever, no matter how hard I try.

I can do one.

And then another. And another. And again. However many ones it takes, I can do that.

I take my miracles where I find them. As much as I would appreciate those miracles to be accompanied with flashes of lightening and blaring thunder, choirs of angels singing and doing the tango on the head of a pin, my life-altering truths tend to be much quieter. They certainly help to get me right-sized and breathing. They slow the patter of my heart, quiet the chittering of old voices that whisper lies in sibilant hisses somewhere in my head.

So. I can do one. Then another. I can give thanks for the small miracles and an avatar of God. I can breathe. I can sing with angels, and then I can do one.

Chasing Fireflies

I have been accused, you may be surprised to hear, of being (shall we say) intense. When the observer is being kind. When said observer is being less kind, intensity turns to scary. Too focused, too needy, too there. As a dear friend (one of the kind ones) once said, "Stacey, you never even give people a chance to miss you."

So, I had a revelation the other day. No; angels did not dance on the head of a pin, and the earth did not move, but I think I figured something out. It has to do with that intensity thing (I was going to say character defect, but I have decided to be a bit kinder to myself) (because I'm nothing if not compulsive and easily distracted by bright shiny objects) (my thoughts mostly shiny and always bright) (and speaking parenthetically to illustrate my distraction). As I was about to say, before I was distracted: on to my rambling revelation - on to INTENSITY.

Here's the deal. For what felt like a thousand years, but turns out to be merely a couple of decades, I lived in a very tiny, tiny universe of one. Nothing got in. Nothing got out. I had decided, somewhere around the time I started drinking, that I could not afford to be hurt again. Life was way too painful. My heart was already quite fragile, and so I wrapped my fear and my anger and my hurt around me like a shield. And I lived that way (ok, "lived" is only an approximation; I was much more like Gollum eventually became - stretched) for a long time. It was... safe.

At least, that's what I told myself. I ignored the leaks, of course. I ignored the seepage of hurt, the numbness of anger, the whisper of pain that managed to find every chink and crack in my carefully crafted armor. They were all brief, flashes of something felt more in retrospect, when I was tired or hungry. It was a lonely and stretched thinner-than-air existence, Of course, the more I drank, the more I took refuge in alcohol-as-shield, the lonelier and more tired I would get.

And then, miracle of miracles - I got sober! And after a little bit of time (Days? Weeks? A year or two? Who the hell knew? Who the hell cared?!) - after a while, I noticed the walls of my tiny little universe of one had crumbled.

The trumpet had blared under the light of a new sun, and I stood before God and everyone else, defenseless and open.

And it was good.

Ok, mostly it was good. I still have my moments, even twenty years and more later, still want to cling to the dark and comforting fog of that particular prison. But God, I was out! I was free. And I could run, and you know what? It feels like I am twirling in a starlit field, twirling and dizzy - not drunk, but alive and dizzy - and chasing fireflies. And I think, really and truly, when I stop to think at all, that this is the feeling that everyone has, all the time. This is the thing I missed for so long! This abandon and exuberance and energy. This is my shout: *Hineini*! Here I am, free at last, in the light of a new day. Let's play! And I really believe that everyone wants to play, to feel that dizzy, twirly, joyous thing.

Nothing is filtered anymore. All I ever did in my old half life was filter: edit, erase, delete, change, hide, scorn, disdain. Take your pick. Everything went through layer after layer of subterfuge until it (whatever "it" was) lay dead at the feet of my metaphor. But not anymore. There are no filters. And that is the source of this intensity. I just want to play. I don't ever want to lose sight of that joy, that connection, that sense that once I was alone and now I am not. I was so alone, for so very long. I have no real frames of reference on how to be not alone. What I get is connection, this electric feeling of not alone.

I know, I know: I have to learn how to put the filters back on. Not in the way they were. Never that. But in a new way, a way that lets the light in still, but that doesn't frighten anyone either. Not an easy task. Certainly not for me, because I like the dizzy, twisty, firefly-catching dance. But I have to learn to temper it. I have to grow up a bit and learn to walk a bit and I can't keep dancing. Can I?

And so there's my revelation. It's just that there are so many fireflies to catch, and I don't want to miss a one. I want to play in that light, the dizzying, twirly light and feel connected. In the end, I am convinced it is the connections that matter - deep and rich and life-affirming. Forgive me as I stumble through my intensity, looking for the filters that mute the intensity to bearable levels.

In the meantime, thanks for letting me dance.

Anniversary

I was coming up to an anniversary – seventeen years sober that August of 2009. There are drinks that hadn't been invented yet when I stopped. In all that time, I have fallen in love, fallen out of love, gotten married, gotten divorced, had cats, given up cats, had a baby and watched him grow. People have lived and died and wandered in and out of my life. I have done the same in many of theirs. I have moved: physically, spiritually, emotionally. I have been lost and found and left and recovered. I am not the same person I was.

My God! Seventeen years. Had you asked me, as I sat on that beat up old couch in that beat up old AA club, crying and tense and scared and lost - had you told me then that this is where my life would have be - I would have thought you were crazy. I couldn't see where my life would be in seventeen minutes, let alone seventeen years. While I may have understood all the words you used individually, I would not have had any clue when you strung them together into a cohesive statement of what I would achieve during those years: love, friendship, trust, feeling, motherhood and recovery.

Of course, I may just have thrown up at that point, whether from fear or being hung over. Take your pick; I think I've finally realized, after all this time, that there is little difference between the two.

Seriously: it's taken almost seventeen years to learn that fear is just like a hangover. Or, at least, fear is what drove me to crawl inside a bottle and set up camp there for a few thousand years. Fear wrapped its icy fingers around my heart at a young age: fear of failing, fear of success. Fear of being alone or unloved or wrong or not enough or too much. I was so sure that *everyone but me* got The Rule Book (at birth, or maybe earlier), and so knew, effortlessly, everything that I didn't. And that lack of knowledge was going to kill me. Or expose me for the fraud that I was - which was a fate worse than death.

The first time I drank, it was as if I could breathe for the first time in my life. I felt that vodka (mixed with grape kool-aid, a combination I learned that very day to stay away from) burn a trail of fire down my pre-teen throat and I knew I was home. Finally. The noise stopped. The fear was driven to the smallest corners of my head, held at bay by that burning, heady liquid. And I felt dizzy and free and I loved it all. And I wanted it. More. And again. Just as intense. Just as powerful. Just as liberating.

And I spent the next couple of decades chasing that same thing. Not surprisingly, I never found it. Not for lack of trying, mind you. It seems, though, that the harder I chased, the more elusive it became. And one day, just about seventeen years ago, I realized the chase was done. I was done.

And here is where I get stuck. How to explain the glory and the struggle and the raw and the sacred of the last seventeen years? It has been all those things and more. I have embraced my life, cursed it, prayed for a soft landing and a softer heart. I have found God, lost friends, restored my credit and ravished it all over again. I paid rent, mostly on time. I paid my mortgage, mostly on time. I paid off debt and created a whole new pile of bills. I finally realized nobody wants my money; they all just want theirs. I learned to feel: to laugh and cry and fear and love. My God! I learned how to love! To open my heart and allow myself to be vulnerable and open and trusting. And still I have been hurt. And still I have hurt. I am intense and impatient and naive. I have looked for redemption and I have found forgiveness.

I stumble and I doubt and I struggle. But I have learned to dance along the edge of my pain, put one foot in front of the other. I remember to breathe, even when I am most afraid. I sing, even when I am most lost.

I have learned that it is not what I pray that is important; it is that I pray. And I pray, every day. I talk to God, and yell and whine and demand and plead and, softly, in the small of night, when it is dark and lonely and cold (because it can still be all of those things, and more), when I can taste the ghost of liquid fire again, when my fear coils like a lover around me and whispers my secret shame - I find God all over again, and I remember to ask for help, and I find some small measure of grace.

I have been given such gifts! And so I laugh, in the midst of my fear. And so I love, in the heart of my solitude. And so I live, in the hope of joy.

Simple Stories

You'd think that after 20 years, this would be easy.

Well, maybe not *you*, but *I* did. *I* thought that after 20 years it would be easy to tell the story of these past 20 years. I am, after all, a writer. I do the words. That's my thing. More than most other things, I know how to tell the stories - some filled with wonder and delight, some much harder, all twisty and dark-cornered, with frayed threads, but which, with infinite and practiced patience, can be woven together into a threadbare whole until a new story can be found. Sometimes wonder, sometimes hard and tinged with light.

You'd think, after 20 years - of living this life and mending all these frayed and broken threads, of finding purpose and dancing with God, of unimaginable pain and unbounded joy - of living this life, actually living a life filled to the very edges with *life*, with everything: love and anger and doubt and fear, failure and triumph, all the stuff of a life jammed together and barely contained - you'd think...

So why isn't this easier?

Why is it so difficult to strip away the artifice and just tell the story, spare and unadorned and achingly simple? Why can't I just say: There was a time, a long time ago, when time was stuck, when nothing moved and nothing changed and nothing filled me and everything failed me. And this is the story of how that all changed.

I was taught, early on in Alcoholics Anonymous, that when you tell your story, you say what it was like, what happened, and what it's like now. Simple.

So, what was it like? I like to believe that that's where the story takes a sharp left turn away from simple, passing complicated in a few easy strides, never looking back. That's the story I tell myself. I like the drama of that, the hint of darkness and the veiled promise of lurid disarray. As comfortably as I live in that drama, I remember what a friend told me one night, early in our sobriety, as we sat in my car under cover of a midnight sky, just learning the rules of friendship in a sober world. I told him my stories through the lens of my living chaos theory. And my dear Jonathan, my new and newly sober friend, he listened, allowed me to rant, took my hand when I'd finished and said "Stacey; you're not as evil as you think you are." I may have hated him in that moment.

That's the thing, really: I *want* complex. I want drama and license and chaos. But the simple story, the easy story is this: There was a time when I was empty, and in my emptiness, time stood still. No light. No sound. Just an eternity of empty. Who needed chaos when I had despair? Who needs hope when you can chase *more* - more *anything*, take your pick: alcohol, drugs, sex, money. Strange, but no matter how much I drank, the empty never got filled. All the despair, all the hopelessness, untouched. Untouchable. An infinite void fed by subtraction stew.

And after twenty years of forever, twenty years of standing motionless on a roiling sea of empty, I was done. That's the "what happened" part. I was done: I got sober. Easy - got sober. Ha! Just don't drink, right? Easy? How the hell do I do that?.

They told me, those people in the rooms, from their vantage points of a decade, a year, a day, an hour of sobriety "Don't drink and go to meetings." Don't drink? What? How do you not drink? How do you not chase that thirty seconds, where you finally sit in your own skin without feeling the need to crawl out of it, that singular instant of time where all the noise in your head stops and you can breathe, really just breathe? Thirty seconds - that's all you get, ever. Thirty seconds, where you fit and the gears don't grind against you and you can just be. And God, what I wouldn't give - what I *didn't* give - to chase those thirty seconds, again and again, with every sip. Don't drink? How the hell do you do that?

And they all of them smiled, and they nodded, and they knew - all of them, from their lofty vantage point of a decade or three, a day or two, an hour or so - "Don't drink. Go to meetings. It gets better. Simple."

I used to not believe in miracles. I used to believe that God, if God really existed, had set me up to fail my life. I used to believe that I couldn't live a life without drinking.

It's amazing the changes that happen when you finally can't imagine having to take one more drink. It's amazing how the universe shifts when the pain of drinking becomes more than the fear of not. How profoundly simple life became: don't drink. Again and again, one second, one minute, an hour or three, and you just don't drink. No matter how much the pain of sobriety threatens to swallow you whole; no matter how exposed and raw you feel - every minute of every day, with not even an ounce of anything standing between you and the rest of the world; no matter how much you're tweaking and want to crawl inside that bottle.

Again and again: don't drink, go to meetings, and the seconds crawl into minutes and stumble into days and bound into years and you suddenly have time. And you breathe, finally breathe. My God, you *breathe* and the air is cool and pure and fills your lungs like light. You breathe, and suddenly you have a life, that moves and leaps and dances. And you look back, and it's twenty years later. Twenty years, and you say: simple.

And now? Now I have a life. A life by no means simple or easy; it wouldn't be mine if that were the case. It is a complex and rich tapestry that is filled to its very edges with life - with love and light and pain and hope. There has been despair enough to fill a thousand lifetimes, and hope enough to bring me to a breathless stop. I have been given gifts unimaginable. I have sought redemption and been offered forgiveness. I have learned to live with doubt, and revel in contradiction. I live in the miracle of a day, a day that stretches before me with infinite possibility and endless hope, filled with simple stories waiting to be found and told and lived, I have found a life that is mine, that moves and breathes and is filled with all the stuff of a life. I have found God, and I allow God to be. Just be, just as I believe God allows me to just be.

There was a time, a long time ago, when time was stuck, when nothing moved and nothing changed and nothing filled me and everything failed me. And this is the story of how that all changed. This is the story of how it got better. This is the story of how I came to believe that I was never empty. This is the story of how I learned to breathe.

Simple.

The Empress of Forever

Invariably, I just up and go to live in the Land of Forever. I am, perhaps, the Mayor there. Or the Empress. I like the ring of that - Empress of Forever. All I need is my tiara and sash, and I'll be set for, well, forever.

Do you know the place?

Forever is the place I go - *always* - when Something Happens. It's always a capital letter event: a Loss, a Disappointment, some Painful Experience. Something that leaves me a little breathless, a little lost, a little twisty. Something Happens and I pack up, riding the train to Forever, where I set up camp and plant myself, to wait Forever. It's a bad neighborhood, Forever is: burnt-out buildings, tumbleweeds, and a howling, keening wind that wraps around my heart and gets under my skin until I want to crawl out of it. Instead, I wrap myself in the armor of memory. Like an endlessly looped movie, I watch the scenes of my pain again and again. There is no surprise at the climax, only a certain kind of inexorable inevitability. There is comfort of a kind in that inevitability.

And I sit. And I wait. And I stay. Forever.

This is what happens, almost always. Almost every time, until the next time, and I don't know when I leave Forever, or how I get back - but I do. I re-enter the world of happy and frustrated and joyous and bills to pay and dinner to cook and life to live. From temporal stasis to moving at the speed of life in a heartbeat, a breath, unnoticed.

Except not this time. For the first time, I am not moving to Forever. For the first time, I seem to have made a side trip to the land of Used To Be. It's an oddly jarring journey.

I don't go anywhere. I still wander through my life and dance to its syncopated rhythms. I cook and clean and watch and write, but in the quiet, offhand moments, when I allow the busyness of my life to still for a stuttery step, Used To Be comes sidling in through some back door, grabbing my attention in the corners and the almosts: almost asleep, almost awake, just out of sight, around the next bend. Almost but not quite vulnerable. Or guarded (which is sometimes, almost, the same thing): I used to be. I used to look. I used to feel. *I used to*

The particular verb escapes me. Or perhaps, it's all of them. An infinity of Used To Bes.

I hear the whispers of that empty, soulless land as a death knell - what once was is no more and will never be again. I used to be younger. I used to be thinner. I used to be pretty. I used to...

I can't seem to find my way out of this place. All I can see, all I can feel, all I want is what used to be.

And perhaps, because it is early August, and the day before the twenty-second anniversary of my getting sober, I have just enough strength, just enough faith and hope to be able to breathe in Now for just a second. To be present, in this moment, and so, remember a few other Used To Bes.

I used to be drunk. If not all the time, then a lot of it. And if I wasn't drunk, then I was cleaning up the mess of my life that came as a result of being drunk. Or attempting to clean it up. More often than not, whatever I tried to fix, or manage or control just got me deeper into my brokenness.

I used to live in a tiny universe of one - lonely and isolated and silent: deathly, desperately silent. There was no you, there was no me, there was no God. Just a vast eternity of empty. I remember the cold of that. I remember slowly dying of that. I used to huddle in on myself, unable to move, to think or feel. I crawled inside a bottle, my shield against pain. I wanted to sink into the liquid courage of that drink. I would cling to my despair as if it could save me - or drown me. I don't think I really cared which. I used to survive - barely - and used to fool myself that drinking would make everything just Stop.

I used to be dying - a sip, a drink, a bottle at a time. I lived in a Forever with no pause. No return. One stretched and attenuated Forever that never changed. I used to think that was okay.

And then, one day, twenty-two years ago, it wasn't okay anymore and I got sober.

One day, twenty-two years ago, the pain of drinking was greater than the fear of not drinking. I slipped free of that universe of one. I left the desolation of my prison, and entered a world of sound and light and motion. There was still pain. There was still fear. But there was joy, too. And grace. And living. There was *living* to do - and I got the bills and the cooking and the cleaning and the driving and schlepping and loving and loosing and grieving and laughing. I got it all. Every breath, every whisper. These days, I even get to take a trip, every so often, to Forever, to set up camp and sit and wait, in silence and in pain - but those trips got shorter every time. The distance between that Eternity and this Now has been bridged. The path is still narrow, and sometimes dangerous, but it's been lit by an infinity of hearts, and there are hands to hold in the darkness while I learn to navigate its sometimes twisty, sometimes merely curved pathways.

And so I move from the harshness of Used To Be to a soft and reverent remembrance: for every Used To Be that I mourn, there are a thousand blessings for all that I have been given. Now is a fine time to be living. Now, not what was, nor what might be, but now, an eternal moment of grace and gratitude.

Faith and Meaning

A celebration of family and community, life and death

I revel in questions – Who am I? How do I fit? Where is God? How do I get closer, draw nearer, rise, even as I despair? Answers let me live in my head. Questions remind me that I live in a community. Faith allows me the grace to find rest and love along the way.

There is something
thrilling
and hesitant
and slightly
off-centered
tender
in the act of saying:

I know you;
at least, I think I do.
We have collided
somewhen,
neverwhere,
and burst into
ribbons of delight
and danced.

And it has just been
until now,
this very moment,
that we have caught
each other's eye
enough to remember
that
I know you,
and have met your heart
before.

Choreography in Holy Time[2]

When my son was born, I cradled him against my heart, arms wrapped gently yet surely around his small and fragile body. I would stand, holding him, our breaths mingled, our hearts beating in an elegant call and response, one beat to the next, and I would sway, a slow and gentle side-to-side rock that lasted for the eternity that exists between heartbeats. I could feel his body relax into the motion, like oceans, like drifting, like peace. I loved the simplicity of that rhythm, the warmth of him, the smell of his newness and his infinite possibilities. As he drifted, as he gentled, my own body would react in kind, and I followed him.

These moments became our own Fibonacci sequence: the delicate curve of our bodies, in motion, at rest, in motion again, twined in an eternal spiral, more intimate than a lover's kiss, repeated again and again and again (world without end, amen).

So, when I found God again -

No. When I found the need to find a *communal* God -

No again: *When I found the need to be part of a community in order to engage and have a conversation with God as* part *of that community, I began to pray more formally.* I began, as it were, to *daven*. In earnest.

It started with Friday nights, happy, joyous celebrations that welcomed in the Sabbath Bride. With music and prayer (and clapping, with an occasional crash of cymbal or the downbeat of a drum), we ushered in Shabbat, remembering the light of creation, the promise of wholeness and completion. I needed the community raucousness, the loud holiness of *erev* Shabbat to ease me into a different kind of worship. My voice was rusty after years of disuse; there was comfort in the foot-stomping, toe-tapping, almost giddy prayer of those nights.

Saturday mornings came later for me, when I learned how to be still, when I learned that listening was as much a part of prayer as words and song. They were all about quiet joy. Intense, but soft and gentle. If Friday nights were

---

[2] This essay was first published by **Lilith Magazine** in a slightly different form, under a different title: "Not Your Grandfather's Shuckle," Summer Issue, 2013

all a communal romp at play in the fields of the Lord, Saturdays and festival mornings were a way to find individual sacredness in the midst of a holy community.

As I prayed, as I found my voice, something surfaced for me. It was so familiar, a recognition that washed over me like pools of light: warm and gentle and cleansing. As a child, I had seen my grandfather *daven* often enough. In *shul*, he and his congregation would *shuckle* as they *davened*, a quick, rhythmic motion back and forth, as if they were all about to walk forward but were rooted in their places. The more impassioned their prayer, the faster they moved. Now, decades later, I found an odd connection to my grandfather: a choreography in holy time. Prayer moved me, not just emotionally, but physically as well.

There was a difference, though. Where my grandfather rocked, forward and back, so ready to be propelled outwards, or upwards, to soar wherever it was that his prayer led him, my dance was different. Mine was that gentle sway, the side-to-side rhythm I had found in my son's infancy. Unlike the *shuckling* of my grandfather's generation, my sway seemed to be centered, to be grounded. Don't get me wrong: one was not better than the other. Just different. I was not meant to be propelled, but to flow. Like oceans or time. Like light.

I cannot shake the feeling that there is something holy in that movement. I can lose myself in that tidal sway, let the sacred wash over me and through me. I can believe, in those moments, that the movement itself, that easy to-and-fro, is a prayer.

I know that it is: sacred and holy and eternal. Like oceans or time. Like light.

Like love.

My son is preparing to become a Bar Mitzvah. To be fair, he is a Bar Mitzvah, having passed his thirteenth birthday just last month. But in fine American Jewish tradition, he is preparing to lead a service, chant from Torah, teach us something about what he chants. As I've tried to teach him, now, not only does the community have something to offer him, he now has something to offer the community. It's a two-way street, and he has obligations to fulfill as he steps onto the path of burgeoning adulthood.

But as he prepares, I've really tried to stay out of it. I'm his mom: I drive him to his tutor's, I remind him to practice (I remind him again to practice), I nag him a little about practicing, I'm planning the social festivities of the day itself (and thinking a lot about wardrobe. Mine, not his.) But I am not his teacher - not for this. Let others help him prepare. I have, I hope, laid the foundation and given him guidance enough for him to follow his own path. But there is a community upon whom he can depend, who have so much to teach and share with him. Let him learn this lesson as well (I pray).

So I was surprised one day, when I reminded him, but had not reached the level of nagging at him, to practice, and he asked if I would chant with him. Would I chant with him? Would I pray with him? Would I?

I held as still as I knew how, as if a delicate butterfly had lit upon my finger, shyly flapping its gossamer wings, so ready to take flight again. I held my breath and nodded, hoping I appeared calm and nonchalant, while inwardly doing my little happy-dance-of-joy. I did not want to frighten him away.

Would I pray with him?

And he came to me while I sat at the table, my not-so-tall boy, my almost man. He came and stood and nestled his body next to mine, so that our hearts beat in time together, a gentle call and response. And we prayed, my son and I, and we swayed, he cradled next to me, a simple back and forth, that gentle back and forth, slow and stately, a dance in holy time. Like oceans, like time. Like light.

Sacred and holy and eternal, like love. Exactly like love.

Time and Light

We mark time, don't we? We mark it and measure it, witness and remember.

"How many sleeps, Mommy?" This from my son, when he was young- too young- to understand divisions of time smaller than a sleep. It was a time when "Five Minutes" meant "some Time not now."

When, Mommy? When?

Five minutes, baby.

It could have been five minutes, five hours, five weeks- it never mattered. It was an acknowledgement that there was a Now and a Not Now.

We still measured it, that Not Now, still marked its passage in some way. Six sleeps until we go to the zoo. Until Chanukah. Until your birthday. Until... It was time, marked and measured. And seemingly, in a moment, sleeps became days, became weeks or months. He could live in those bigger divisions, feel the passage of time differently. I miss the grand and easy sweep of time, as much as I miss counting those sleeps.

Milestones. They are the remembered days, the points that mark the linear drift of our lives, the divisions of time that don't fit inside a watch, and barely fit inside a calendar. They are witnessed and measured, because it matters- desperately matters- upon which side of those milestones we stand.

Before that marked and measured event, we are one way, we see the world this way, we are perceived that way. We act and we choose and we do in the Before, until magically, we are on the other side, privy to a whole new set of choices and expectations and commitments. There is an infinity of possibilities, a singularity of difference, until it too, this milestone in time, gets lost and dusty and fuzzy around the edges, and we discover the next one; until it, too, gets measured and marked and remembered, until one day, we move on, we turn from remembrance to anticipation.

And so it goes. Time is marked, and measured. Events are witnessed. And we are changed by it all.

I've had my share of marking time this year. With each measure, I have been changed in some way. There have been celebrations of new beginnings and the fiftieth anniversary of my birth. There have been remembrances and mourning for things let go. Holidays have been marked. Time has passed, and we – I - have stood witness to it all, sometimes on the banks of that mighty river, passively watching it go by, sometimes right in the middle of the stream, splashing in the waters of those events, those celebrations, those milestones.

Nothing big. Nothing earth-shattering in its import. Small events, gently flowing streams of time that separate the Before from the After. But I measure their passage, and mark them. I was both witness and participant in the same breath. Here, on this side, was one world. And suddenly, the horizon tilts and there is a brand new world, a subtle shift in color and light laid out before me, waiting to be discovered and savored.

Next month it will be my turn to witness another milestone: my son will turn thirteen. Thirteen! We, both of us, will mark it and measure it and be changed by this day. He will not be a man. He will be... himself. A newer, more self-assured, more questioning, older, thoughtful, mindful, analytical, brash and playful self. Already he is leaping, with faltering grace. Already he is drinking in information and ideas and thoughts and is drawing his own borders, making his own connections. Already his logic is more sound, his conclusions more sure than what came seemingly moments before.

He stands now, poised on the edge of time, already gathering himself, already testing those waters, feeling the sharp and chill exhilaration of the new and different and exciting, tasting the sweetness of the yet-to-be. Where will he stand, on the other side of this day, that will make a difference, that will change him?

He will not be a man; not yet. He will travel many miles and pass through many years before he can claim that, before he will be shaped into a man. He will be a boy still, caught so delicately between an infinity of worlds. And yet he will be changed. He will be different. Time will have shifted, separating one moment from the next, creating an infinite vista of the possible. In an instant, on that day, he will cross the divide of time and stand on the shoulders of giants and wrap himself in a garment of light and loose thread and bind himself to his past and his future.

My son, my beloved boy, will stand with me on the Shabbat of his thirteenth birthday. I will be his witness, as he offers ancient words of blessing and praise, as he takes my Grandfather's *tallit* and places it gently on his broadening shoulders. He will wind the fringes around his fingers and gather the threads into a whole. His will be a new song, a new dance, a new celebration. His will be a new voice in the wilderness, and our sacred and holy community will be all the richer for it. He will begin to find his own way, journey on in solitary wonder, in companionable joy, in defiance and innocence and doubt.

We measure time, don't we? Measure it and mark it, witness and remember. Here, on the edge of his childhood, the border of a distant shore, he will remember this moment, he will mark the not-Now and measure the Yet-to-be. From this day forward, he will stand, ever and always, cloaked in light and gathering loose threads into a new whole.

My son, my beloved boy, will leap into the infinite and he will soar.

Fringes[3]

I don't remember my childhood. At least, not in any contiguous pattern, a fluid arc of cause and effect, with beginnings and middles and ends. There is no cosmic projector whirring and spinning through dusty light, flashing a story line - neither love story nor horror film nor some tender coming of age film - on some interior screen, while I sit on a worn plush seat, a spring pushing against the small of my back and the butter from my popcorn making my fingers shiny with grease, while I watch, rapt.

There's not even a vague disinterest as I view my life as if it were someone else's story I were viewing from some distant, disconnected height. There's no boredom, or sadness or wistful hope. There are just huge patches of not much of anything - no dust bowl and tumbleweeds, no darkness and a keening, plaintive wind, none of those common tropes.

No trope, and no memories, although, if you ask my mother, she'd say I just remember the bad stuff. That may be truer, if truth can have a comparative, a greater than or lesser than finality. It's not that I have no memories. It's not that I only remember The Bad Stuff, cataloging all the pains and hurts and disappointments of childhood for later review and recrimination. There was love and joy and frustration and sad and wonder and love and pain, over and over and over again. It was all the warp and weft of our family.

But I don't have those stretches, those seamless and flowing pictures of time and love. Or of pain. What I have, I realized, is picture frames - brief flashes of color and light that surprise me and take me off guard in a disjointed array.

The frames of my father are mostly small. There's the color of his coffee – a rich caramel that steamed against the unnatural whiteness of a Styrofoam cup. There's a feathered headdress, worn in the days before political correctness, as he and my big brother who was all of seven or eight, but he was so much bigger than I, and older, and closer to my dad, who came home from the office, tired and spent, but who could muster up just enough energy and attention to do Indian Guides with my brother, and who promised we'd do Indian Princesses when I got older.

---

[3] This essay was written for Craig Taubman's *Jewels of Elul: The Art of Return*, Volume 10. 2014

There's the stats book for the Little League teams he managed, first for my older brother, who started young and in the outfield – right field, the home of lost players who hadn't yet gotten the hang of the game and so were placed there, where they could do little harm – and who got better, year after year, all the way through the Pony Leagues. He coached my younger brother the year of the locusts, whose carapaces littered the ground and made walking noisy and slightly disgusting. I kept the stats every season, even the Year of the Locusts, so that I could sit next to my father on the bench, so that I could tag along into his world of sports and sons and attention. It wasn't Indian Princesses, but it was a place near him and so I hoped that it would be enough.

There's the frame that holds the picture of my brother, standing between my father's legs, his hands clutching my father's and a look of gleeful terror on his face as my father lowered him slowly. "Keep your arms stiff. I won't drop you!" he would say to my brothers, who both couldn't wait to play this heady and terrible game of Trust, as it was called in our family parlance. A simple game – how low could you go, how close to the floor could you go, with only our father there to hold you, keep you from falling and crashing to the floor. I would watch in envious and eager anticipation for my turn, so sure that this time, please this time, I would have the courage to play.

There is one frame, though, one small picture that is mine alone. Mine and my father's. It is the picture of us, sitting together in *shul*, so close that I could feel the wool of his suit against my face and arm, sheltered by his nearness, carried gently by the drone of his voice as he prayed in a language that was at once familiar and strange, and the cadence of his chanting lulled me. He would hold me close, his arm wrapped around my shoulder and his *tallit* covering me. Sitting there, sheltered, I would play with the fringes of his *tallit*, wrap them around my fingers, stretch them until they lost their elasticity and shape. His hand would cover mine, to still my fidgeting, and it would linger there, tangled with the fringes, connecting us.

These small picture frames of love and longing come, in flashes of light and heat. When I sit with my son, so close that our shoulders bump, and my arm laces through his – because he is too tall for me to wrap it around his shoulder now – and we pray together, in a language at once ancient and new, and my *tallit* shelters us both, my son takes the fringes and he stretches them and tangles them and wraps them in his fingers, these fringes of love.

I return, again and again, to that small picture frame, now large enough to hold us all, to shelter my memory with love and grace.

Joy in the Empty Spaces

I miss my brother. It has been almost a year since he died, and still, there are times when missing him threatens to swallow me whole. In an instant, grief comes racing in from nowhere, and I am wrapped in solitary and breathless sorrow. Mostly though, it is a gentle missing, filled with love and soft regret - that he is gone, that my hand is halfway to the phone before I remember that he won't answer, that he will not see his nephew make that sometimes graceful, sometimes gawky leap from childhood to adolescence to adulthood, that there is a small emptiness where he once stood.

And what if he suddenly appeared, filling that empty space? What would I say?

I have no idea.

I'd like to think that I managed, through grace and luck, to say everything I needed to say before he died. Words like *I miss you* and *I love you* skitter through my head, fleeting as a summer shower. All our words, all our thoughts: spoken and unspoken, whispered and trumpeted in our pain and our hope, they were all woven together within the tight space of his hospital room, connecting him to us to God in some eternal tapestry of unutterable and awesome beauty.

I think. I hope.

I pray.

I've prayed a lot this last almost-year. I stumbled into that sacred dance of mourning, a stutter step of hesitation, growing in surety and ease, reciting such ancient words to the exaltation of a God who seems both near and far, present and not, just and merciful and cruel. In the beginning, I wept - great wracking sobs that stole my voice and my exaltation. I wept - and there were hands that reached out, in comfort and with grace. And when I could not pray, could barely manage to say my brother's name, there were other voices to carry me, to lift me and sustain me and let me find my way.

Reciting *Kaddish* is no longer a staccato pulse, insistent and harsh and pounding. Now there is a quiet grace note, starting low, gaining in depth and richness as I stand with eyes closed and fingers laced around my prayer book. There is such power in this prayer! I can feel my brother, close as light, as heat or love. My sorrow washes over me like water over stone, clean and pure, no longer pooling, dank and cold, at my feet. I can feel God again, holy and waiting for me to start the dance, ready to catch me should I falter.

Just about a year. It has taken me just about a year to find my way to this place of - if not exaltation, then certainly of celebration - of my brother, of God. Even of God.

And now it's time to let my brother go.

Not his memory, or my love for him. Not even of my sadness. All this time - of sorrow and grief and learning to find laughter and joy and hope again, I thought this was his last gift to me, a last lesson: learning to find joy in the empty spaces. Every day, for eleven months, I have recited Kaddish. I have stumbled and stammered my way through these words to honor my brother and his memory, to find grace and healing, to rest again in the palm of God's hand.

Almost a year later, and I finally get that this has been about *his* journey, not mine.

For these eleven months, our mourning has allowed us to share in his soul's journey, to help him find his way. Now he must find that last bit of eternity on his own. This is about his soul's journey - to God perhaps, or to Home, or Heaven. Perhaps everywhere all at once. But it is *his* way to find. We release him, in love and faith, into the sacred space of remembrance.

We say *zichrono liv'rachah:* may his memory be for a blessing. He touched the hearts and lives of so many, and the world is different - better - because he was in it. His memory will surely be a blessing.

But there is one other thing. More than a blessing, let his memory be for a prayer: *zichrono l't'filla.* Let his memory teach us to reach and strive and praise and celebrate and hope and love. Every day. Even as we mourn, perhaps because we mourn, let his memory be for a prayer - of comfort, whole and holy.

What would I say to my brother, if he appeared, if he paused for a moment just before he soars and leaps and dances with God? I would say *I love you; I miss you.* And finally -

Let your soul find peace on your journey.
Let your memory shine as blessing and prayer.
And let us say: amen.
Zichrono liv'rachah v"t'filla

A Quiet and Holy Current

Black tights.

Black knit dress.

Careful makeup, a touch of jewelry and heels. A hooded raincoat, to stave off the gusty downpour of rain and sleet. I grabbed my *kippah* (tastefully black, like everything else I wore) just before I shut the car door. One more funeral, after a handful of funerals in the last month or two.

As I put the clips on, to keep it from slipping off, I heard Nate laughing in my head. Of course he would be laughing. At me. "What are you doing?" he would rasp. "Girls aren't supposed to wear *yarmulkes* (the Yiddish word for *kippah*)!" Then he would throw up his arms - dismissively, I think, when we first met, and then later, more in gentle resignation, while a proverbial "Bah!" slipped out under his breath. Or not so under his breath. He wasn't shy about anything, especially in letting you know exactly what he thought about something.

I had no illusions about what he thought of me. I met him in my mid-forties. I was a girl to him - not because he was thirty-some odd years my senior, but because I was, well - a girl. My gender, the two Xs of my chromosomes declared me to be a girl forever. Not a woman. Not an equal. A mere girl.

And yet, there I was, every Saturday morning, talking Torah with the guys. And praying with them.

And more - I argued (in the best, most philosophical sense of the word) with them, and with the rabbi, too. Sometimes I argued with myself. I disagreed as easily and as often as I agreed. But I was an uppity girl, who had the temerity to talk Torah with the guys, and then stay to pray with them. Every Saturday morning, for years.

It was the best part of my week, every week, for years. Me, and my guys.

They had been coming together for Shabbat morning services for almost as long as I'd been alive. Maybe more. These men, these remnants of a different world and another time - they were the captains of industry, the craftsmen and the doctors, the scientist and industrialists, shop owners and salesmen. They were the symbol of the American landscape writ large, across the small backdrop of our synagogue: mainly second generation Americans who were taught that the rhythm of Jewish life was the undercurrent of everything else. It held them and sustained them and became the bedrock upon which they created and lived their lives.

After a while, when it looked like I wasn't going anywhere, that I was maybe perhaps a regular, they would tell me stories of what it used to be like, when the synagogue was in a different place, a grand old building on another side of town, a growing and thriving and tightly-knit community. Over lunch, they would talk of births and deaths and weddings that arced through the steady stream of *b'nai mitzvah* - boys (with the occasional girl on a Thursday or Friday night) who would make their way to the *bimah* and stand so stiffly in a suit and tie, waiting with a butterfly stomach before leaning over the Torah, with its yellowed parchment and hand-scribed letters, while they, the fathers, simply *kvelled*. It was a life they were making, for themselves and their families, bordered on every side by this holy place.

I don't know that they would have defined it as holy. Not then, when they were young and ambitious and feeling their way in the footprints of their fathers. Then it was bricks and mortar and salaries and schools. There were rabbis to hire and committees to fill and teachers to find. There were leaks to plug and money to be raised. Lots of money - a never-ending stream of money to fund a never-ending stream of fixing and hiring and need. They would get quiet, my guys, my Saturday morning *minyan* guys, and let slip the stories of the time (those many, many singularly repeated times of compassion and humanity and righteousness) when one of their group - nameless, because that's how it worked - who made sure that this one or that one, that kid with the patched clothes or the rumbling stomach, had tuition, or a *bar mitzvah* or a book. Or that his parents could pay dues. Or a car note.

They were a community. They were a family, forged by shared ties and shared faith.

For all of that, time moved and landscapes shifted. While faith might be constant, the synagogue - and the community - morphed, and then morphed again. From Orthodox to Conservative to Reform, moving farther west into different, newer, more modern buildings, this once large and thriving community was changing, growing smaller, more diverse. Faces changed more frequently, custom was lost, traditions changed.

But these men, this Saturday morning *minyan* of men, gathered together, every Shabbat morning, to study and pray and connect. And slowly, like the drift of planets and time, they let me in.

Every week, we would study some, and pray some and eat some. They taught me their rhythms, their quiet. If Friday night services were a joyous, raucous dance with God, Saturday with my guys was an inward journey, a solitary yet shared walk. It was no less joyous, but we seemed to find God in the stillness, in the gentle stream of light that came in through the windows, and the dancing of the dust motes as we moved in a slow and steady cadence through the service. They taught me to listen for God, that listening and quiet and service to others were their own kinds of prayer, and that every prayer was holy.

I was an uppity girl, but they made a place for me, right next to them. I am infinitely blessed to have been able to stand with them, these captains of industry, these men of quiet faith. Every Saturday morning, for years, we stood together, and prayed some and learned some. We celebrated and grieved some, too. We were a family. A community.

I don't know if I ever mentioned how much I loved them. Love them still. They brought a depth and richness and a thousand points of brilliance that had been missing into my life. I was changed because I knew them and loved them. My guys, my Saturday guys. They are fewer now. I am shocked, when confronted once more with the reality of their absence, just how much smaller the group is now. I have had to say good-bye far too many times of late. But we come together, to grieve and remember, to tell stories of our lives and the lives of those for whom we gather. We are carried by the rhythms of faith and love, a quiet and holy current.

Zichronam liv'rachah - may their memories be for a blessing. I carry you with me always, and remember you in the quiet stillness of a Saturday morning, as I listen for the voice of God and find community and benediction there. Thank you for the gift of your lives, the song of your prayers and silence.

And so let us say: Amen

A Cry in the Wilderness

A day after I began writing this essay, my friend's husband lost his battle with cancer. His memory will be a blessing, his life was a prayer. His family will grieve and find comfort in their wilderness. Together they will find healing and learn to be whole again. And let us say: Amen.

My friend's husband is dying. His death is imminent, a matter of days at best.

From the time he was diagnosed, they've had kids to raise, a house to run, meals to cook, carpools to drive. They've helped with homework and changed diapers and created a patchwork quilt made of comfort and stitched with hope. They've experienced great kindness and felt the soul-sucking aloneness of despair. Their family has grown by a glorious one. They've lived their lives, cursed their private hell, leaned on friends, and been surrounded by love. They have seen their children grow and grieve, and have been helpless in the face of that grief.

It has been less than a year.

Not enough time. Never enough time to love and hope and grow and be, to live the life that suddenly seems too crowded with everything that makes up a life.

Not enough, but surely more than enough time to curse at God, raise holy hell. Enough time, enough bewilderment to demand to know just where the hell God is in all of this.

"Screw you, God," we cry out into the wilderness of our pain. Who, in the face of such cruel and capricious reality has not railed against it? We are taught the laws of cause and effect from the time we can begin to comprehend the magnitude of this seemingly immutable law. It is a cosmic law, this if....then equation, a calculus of horrible consequences.

I know that place, that cursing, angry, defiant and terrified place. I have wept and wondered at the why of this despair. I have demanded answers from a silent God. I am good, mostly. And kind. I follow the rules, and color inside the lines. Mostly. Where's the reward for my (mostly) decent and very human life? Why am I being punished? Was I not good enough? Did my life not measure up?

Answer, dammit. Tell me. Nothing? Silence, still? Well then, God: screw you. Go to hell.

And there, in the darkness of my despair and pain, my greatest prayer: *Screw you, God*. I am convinced that this, too, can be the healing grace of God. Blessing and curse. I have been blessed; I have been cursed. It depended less upon God and more upon my perception. I believe that God needs to hear our raw, unvarnished anguish. I believe that God needs to hear our pure and unadulterated joy. I believe they are one and the same thing.

It is not what we pray that matters. It is, ever and always, *that* we pray.

How could we not? Underneath our cursing, do we not find the unspoken prayer *do not forsake me, God; do not abandon me to my pain!* The Psalmist had it right: we cry out to God and we are healed. He didn't say *what* we cried, or how. He didn't tell us "God only hears the beautiful, pretty words. Speak only of love and praise. Only then will you be heard." No. It's pretty clear: we find healing *because* we cry out in our anger and our fear.

Blessing and curse. God does not screw with us. We are neither abandoned nor forgotten nor ignored. Neither does God bestow presents upon us: we do not get parking places or jobs, nor do we win ballgames or wars as a result of our prayers. What we get, simply, is grace. What we get is strength and courage to face what life has placed in front of us in that moment. My faith will not guarantee that I will never know fear again, or that only good things will happen. My faith, my prayer, my continued conversation with God allows me to put one foot in front of the other, and know that I will be carried through.

And God. Where is God in all of this? God is there, on my sidelines, waiting, with infinite patience, infinite compassion, for me to remember to cry out. God waits, to give me grace, to turn my mourning into dancing. God waits to dance with me.

The Sound of Your Voice

We are commanded to hear. Of course, the commandment, as I read it, is more about "Listen up - something really important is coming, that you need to hear," I take it to heart: Listen. Hear. And I hear everything. All day, every day, there is a lot of noise out there, and it doesn't stop. And every noise seems to proclaim "Listen up! Hear me!" and I do.

I want it to stop, yet I am afraid of the quiet. And so it goes: a constant barrage of noise, from soothing to seething and reeling and roiling, there is an eternal psalm of noise that needs to be - yearns to be - longs to be heard.

I dwell in the distraction of all that noise.

There are times I hear better than others. I can hear my child laugh from a great distance. I can hear him weep or cry out no matter how loud the cacophony around him is, and I hear his breath at night. I hear him with my heart, where there is no such thing as distance or clutter, just connection.

I tend to hear music, instrumental, piped in, live. Doesn't matter. I'll be sitting with friends over coffee, chattering and fluid, and suddenly hear the faint strains of some piece of music (usually bad elevator music that has no life or pulse in it, and I am grateful when it is not that); "I hate this song," or "I love this song," I will say, and am met with "What song?" *Can't they hear it?* I'm forever amazed that the music goes unnoticed, unheard. But *I* hear it. I am witness to the notes that play.

I am woken by dump trucks, startle at sirens, calm at bird song and get lost in the sound of water. I have found God in the sound of the waves that lick and jump and tangle with the shore.

I am commanded to hear, and so I do.

There is one sound that I look for, strain for, miss more than anything: my father's voice. I didn't love it. There was no special resonance in it. He was a baritone - the in-between pitch of Everyman. Normal. Pleasant. He sang beautifully, but I don't remember his songs, or his voice when I reach back into the memory banks of my childhood. He sang Barber Shop in a choir years later, long after he had moved to Memphis. It was his joy, his love, his retreat after the long hours he sat on the Federal Bench. He often sent me CDs of his performances. They went unlistened to; I am not a fan of Barber Shop quartets.

And please - don't misunderstand! My father hasn't died. He is just voiceless. Two years ago, in order to treat the cancer that had invaded his throat and voice box and tongue, the doctors performed a trachyectomy. They removed his voice box in exchange for saving his life. We are all good with that.

But I miss my father's voice, even though I can't seem to remember just what the hell it sounded like.

He has a mechanical voice now. As my son, much younger then, dubbed him - Robot Zayde. It is painful and difficult for him to speak. So, he doesn't talk much. Not that he ever did; he disliked talking on the phone, answered questions with an economy of words that astounded me (considering my motto is "why use ten words when a hundred will do?). He is quiet. He is content. All good.

A few nights ago, I had a house full of people. Sadly, we had all gathered to sit *shiva* for my mother's brother, my Uncle Phil. While I have thrown myself into my Judaism over the last handful or two of years, searching and stumbling around, looking for meaning, looking for God, my family has not. At my bat mitzvah forty years ago (oy!), I called my parents "lox and bagel Jews." Not much has changed since then. While holidays are celebrated gastronomically, they tend to avoid the more formal expressions of Judaism. When my son became a *bar mitzvah* a few years ago, although they couldn't manage to make it to the synagogue on Friday night, at least everyone was there on Saturday morning. And so it goes: we have all taken a different path to God.

Shiva was what it always has been for me – a celebration of life, a time to mourn and remember and find strength in community. If I – *when* I falter, I am caught, ever and always. It is, to me, the best of who we are, this uncompromising demand that no one ever grieve alone. So the house was noisy and crazy and full to the brim. Even that day, the day my uncle was buried, there was a coming together that made sure we each of us knew we were not alone.

The *minyan* service seemed to take its cue from the day: quiet, hesitant, leaning in and reaching up to one another. Hebrew and English mixed and twisted together, forming a tight bridge, or a handhold – something to grab onto. The air and the walls buzzed with softly droning chants, as people murmured and mumbled their way through the evening service. We made time for words, and then time for silence.

As we came out of that silent meditation, my friend began to play the familiar chords to *Oseh Shalom*, creating her own bridge between prayer and memory. And into that holy space, of peace and wholeness, my father brought his hand up to the mechanical device that allows him to breathe and speak, and he sang with us. "I am here;" he sang, "hear my voice – I am with you, and moved by you, strengthen you and find comfort in you."

I am so grateful that I was able to be a part of that sacred moment, a part of that song. It was not the voice I remembered, my father's harsh, mechanical and flat voice. It was much more beautiful than anything I've ever heard.

Blessing and Pain

I spent most of the day at the hospital, talking about really uncomfortable things.

If the heart stops, do we try to start it again? This has nothing to do with a broken heart, but a beaten, barely beating one. *What then? If the heart doesn't quite stop, but falters, what then? How much do we try to restore it?*

And what about an invasion, not of soldiers or marauders (or at least, not in any human form), but microscopic ones, who invade the blood and infect the body. Do we fight them off? Do we go bravely into battle until they are routed, every last one of them?

When do we stop trying to... I can't even imagine the proper infinitive that belongs in that blank space. Is it to try, or maybe to will, or to fix and mend and heal and -

Please God, let there be no pain. How about that? Just: no pain.

That's a perfect goal, though it doesn't fall into a tidy infinitive. Right about now, I am hungering for tidy, for neat little boxes that fit, with no lumps or leftover parts.

Thing is, life isn't tidy. At least, not any of the lives I've met. Not now. Not *anywhen*. Not ever. Life is filled with messy, and lumpy and almost-but-not-quite fitting. There is no symmetry, no equal and opposite reaction, no tried and true equation that says "for every Part A of Sadness, add a Part B of Kindness..." Every soul, every life, is a jumble of goodness and meanness and pity and thoughtlessness and grand generosity and fear and glee and on and on. We are human, and so we have within us the seeds of everything imaginable (and a few not so imaginable, maybe, things that, by definition, I cannot even conceive of right now, or then, or ever).

So the man lying in the hospital bed, in the room of the very uncomfortable discussions, was just that: filled with huge generosity and the finer points of cruelty. He was kind and happy and mean and depressed and generous and growing confused. He was in pain and rich in spirit. He loved fiercely and hated with passion. It did not balance. The pendulum swung wildly, less a back and forth and more a whirling gyroscope that spun madly - but it was beautiful and drew your eye.

This is my uncle, whose madly spinning life is starting to wobble and sway and slow. This is my uncle, who is complex and difficult and brilliantly present, and his life is fraying around the edges. This is my uncle, and discussions concerning him are less about healing and more - *Please God, let there be no pain.*

And all the while, today, while we talked, my mother and my cousins and the whole team of caregivers who were present in that room, I could only think that the room was filled with a thousand, thousand blessings.

My uncle is pretty sick. He's dying, in fact. Conversation is no longer about healing, but is laced with words like "palliative" and "comfort" and the alphabet soup of DNRs and POAs. We all hate it. We all love him. We all want to make sure that he's comfortable, that he's getting all the care that he needs. There was a team of caregivers present, to match the team of relatives and loved ones sitting in a small circle of sun and warmth and too-bright light that streamed through those huge windows. We all had a single purpose - let's figure out what this man needs and make sure that we can give it to him.

This man, this human being who has lived his life to the very edges, who is so very human, whose life is messy and whose breath is raspy and harsh and whose arms seem to have shrunk even while his hands have remained so huge - big enough to conquer the world, surely - my uncle sits surrounded by care and concern and love. We cannot save him. We cannot heal him. We can go back and forth and around again about keeping his broken heart beating.

He is surrounded by love.

For all of his pain, for all that his ferocity and great, gawping energy is quieting - he is surrounded by love.

My faith calls me to shift, to change, to turn the kaleidoscope so that the light bends and flows and the jeweled bits dance. Here is my lesson on blessings today: they are all around us, even in the discomforting, uncomfortable parts. There is grace in that, and infinite, boundless love.

Who Brought Us to **This** Moment

Faith, Celebration and the Seasons of Joy

There is such joy in being carried along the river of the year, a rush of straights and eddies and rock-strewn rapids, able to find rest and respite in holy moments – celebrations of God and community and time.

*Praise to You, God
of the infinite and ever,
Of cold and heat,
And leaves of heartbreak gold;
Of the first pale blush of roses,
Of gathering and sowing
And drawing near –
Blessings of life
Blessings of keeping
And carrying
And bringing us all
To this season of Joy*

Week's End, with a Promise

This has been a long week. Lately, they all seem long.

The days push and pull at me, demanding my attention, my devotion, my energy. At the end of the day, when dark gathers in small corners and the noise of the day skitters at the edge of consciousness, I lay, exhausted but wired, willing my mind to calm, to rest, to slow down please God! let it slow down so I can sleep. But I don't. I court sleep like a coy lover. It is elusive, teasing me with a promise of rest, only to run away at the last instant, leaving me tangled in sweat-dampened sheets.

Again and again, I repeat this dance. Eventually I sleep. For a couple of hours, I am at rest. But the alarm rings too early, its shrill buzz shatters the mornings quiet. I am awake, dammit! Really. Pay no attention to the cramped fingers that scritch across the nightstand, seeking the snooze button. I am awake! Buzz, buzz, buzz, incessant and raucous and deafening. Awake, dammit, until silence. Blessed silence. I drift on a sea of in-between: not morning quite yet, but no longer night; neither asleep nor awake, but aware. I just need a few more minutes, hours, days. Please.

And suddenly, it is Shabbat. God's cosmic snooze button. Timeless and in-between, outside and separate. Suddenly, I can breathe. I am at rest.

I love this time of year. I sit in the sanctuary on Friday night, my skin still buzzing with the noise of the week, my head in a million different places everywhere at once, and I watch the light outside the window as it ushers in Shabbat. I cannot see the sun, only its light as it changes, mellows and deepens. The wild grasses are tipped in gold and a single tree, dusty green and brown, gathers shadows under a darkening sky, a slow study in purple and grey and black. The sky goes from the pale blue of a summer day to a luminous cerulean blue.

Shabbat is here at last, the beautiful bride, dancing in from the fields just as surely as the Kabbalists rejoiced a few hundred years ago. It is a celebration, a promise in song and prayer and light. Is it the light of creation? Some have argued it is, that the light of Shabbat is so pure, so perfect, it is the remembrance of creation that shines on us for a brief time. I don't know; I would like to believe it.

My heart is not as calcified, as protected as it once was, when I was angry with God and my only prayer was a quick "screw you." I declared my disbelief in God to any who would listen, and to many who wouldn't. What I didn't share was my secret belief that it was God who didn't believe in me. It has softened, it is not quite so protected these days. God and I are pretty tight, I think. And so, with all my weary heart, I take comfort that Shabbat is a gift, a promise from God: we can rest, we can breathe. We step outside of time, to celebrate, to study, to renew, to listen, to love, to find the sacred, remember the holy.

And for this brief and timeless time, I find rest, I find God, I find peace.

The Holiness of Separation

As a kid, Shabbat meant brisket. I loved that. Every once in a while, my mother would get inspired and feel the need to… cook? No, she always cooked in those days. It wasn't until many years later that dinner was more likely to be ordered than made.

But every so often, as a kid, dinner wasn't just thrown together from whatever was in the refrigerator. Candles were lit. There was no real ritual there, and the melody we used was likely to be the one from Chanukah (because that's the only one I knew, and I was the designated candle-lighter/singer in those days), but those thick, squat white candles that came in boxes of 48 would be given a place of honor on the stove – just in case, because you didn't want them to fall over in whatever tumult might arise after dinner.

My bubbe (z"l), who was either prophet or witch, said to my mother in that distinct and scratchy-voiced Yiddish accent, "You're going to burn the house down with those Shabbos candles," and sure enough, the candles did fall over the next time we lit them. They did a slow burn on the harvest gold Formica countertop, leaving an oddly shaped, flaky mark the size of an orange, or maybe a baseball, as a permanent reminder of her powers – which we kids were never quite certain were always used for good, even though she was our bubbe. Maybe it had something to do with the eyes, or the accent, or her refusal to talk about her life in the before – when she lived in Poland, or Russia, or whichever principality claimed the *shtetl* that was a pawn in skirmishes far removed from the realities of *shtetl* life, but seemed to impact illusory allegiances and political borders.

I am almost convinced that it was because of my bubbes that we celebrated Shabbat at all. And because of their bubbes. And theirs. And theirs again, down a long, dusty and twisted road of generations, a collection of bubbes stretching back a few millennia. It is a small taste of infinity, a forever line, connected by flame and sweet wine, by twisted bread and a thousand generations, all of whom danced on the head of that same sacred pin: a pause, an inward sigh of breath, just as Friday's sun kisses the western horizon. They gather us all in, just as they gather in the light around them, their hands circling over and around the candles they light to usher in Shabbat. Those flames flicker and stretch and reach upwards – to God, to heaven, to separation.

One heartbeat to the next. One moment from the next. An endless next, that leads us all to that sacred space: Shabbat.

They kept it, watched over it, guarded it, remembered it – that liminal moment of joy. And in their watching, in their remembrance, they passed it on, one to the next – one heartbeat, one moment, one candle flame, one breath. Down and down, their fingers wove a prayer, and they gathered us all in. They knew, every one of them, as they stood on the threshold of that endless moment, knew and understood the holiness of separation.

It was not the brisket that made it Shabbat when I was a growing up. What mattered was the separation – the fact that my mother knew, somewhere in her heart and hands, to gather us in and surround a moment. And that moment was separate from, distinct and different from, all the other moments that led up to it. It was space, not time. It was holy, and it was Shabbat.

And for that moment, that breath, that heartbeat, we all of us danced on the head of that pin.

Today? No brisket. But there are candles and flowers, sweet wine and twisted bread. As my hands pass over the small flames, I chant an ancient blessing in an ancient language, gathering in the light, gathering in family and those I hold dear, gathering in hope. I watch, from one moment to the next, and remember, from one heartbeat to the next, and welcome in Shabbat, giving thanks for the holiness of separation.

Psalm 92
A poem for Shabbat

And so we stand
On the edge of this week

Pebbles strewn at our feet
The distance between us an endless heartbeat
The difference like night
Like day
Like light and darkness

Like God
Who separates the days
And brings us
Ever and always
To this holy edge

To this Shabbat

Where we stand
Trembling with effort
Weary from a week filled with
Noise and action and movement
Restless and driven
From one moment to the next
Until we are brought to this edge

This endless and always edge
To this Shabbat
Sacred and at peace
We pause
We breathe
At rest

Separate

Together
With God
Together
With one another
In a flickerflame of candle light
The setting of the sun
From one breath to the next
One heartbeat
We stand on the edge and cross into the infinite
As one
Into peace
Into Shabbat.

Friday Night Kitchen
A poem for Shabbat

Nestled
In the center
Surrounded by the sizzle
and the hiss and the
Plenty

Surrounded by voices and
Steam and flicker flames
Rising
Ascending

A prayer of thanks.

We prepared the banquet
Together
Laid the harvest in fragrant baskets there
Lingered among the sweet and
Liquid smells as the air

Settled
As the sun lowered
And the windows darkened
And the day quieted.

We lingered there
Nestled there
Around that center
Around that heart
And we rested.

And When I Leave

A poem for Havdallah

I am not ready
To leave this place
this time
this rest.
I am not ready
for the separation that
must come, not while
I still smell
the sweetness
of cardamom and cloves.
I want to linger
in this holy time
this sacred promise
And be
Just be.
But the stars are dancing
One
Two
Three
A thousand
Infinity and
More,
They scatter like pebbles
strewn on a field of
velvet night.
And there are numberless shades
of dark,
broken by those infinite and
silvered pebbles.
And oh! my feet ache
to explore that vast expanse,
even as my heart yearns

to stay,
to linger
in this place,
where I can still
taste the wine
that teases my tongue.
But I have blessed
The thin line that
Separates
Dark from
Light,
And Sacred
From Holy.
I have found
Rest and
peace and
comfort
and God.
And when I leave,
Though I ache to linger,
I will take with me
the sweet scent of spice, and
the teasing taste of wine, and
I will hear, Forever
the guttering of a candle
into a cup of wine,
Which will Forever be
the sound of Promise
and the promise of
Return.

Fear, Faith and a Really Big Sea

I'm in one of those places: stuck, prickly, at the very edge of letting go, trembling with the effort to not tip over the edge into the abyss of the unknown, desperate to take that final leap of faith and soar towards light and wholeness. I am astounded, as always, when I think how inextricably intertwined my fear and my faith have become. I have heard (more times than I care to remember) that Fear (always pronounced with a capital F) is an absence of Faith. No. I think not. I demand *Not*. I am too intelligent - God is too intelligent - to demand unthinking. blind faith like that, to insist that faith is a guard against fear.

Faith does not shield me from fear. Rather, it is a guard against inaction. Fear is quite real. There are Monsters, real and scary. Always have been. They hide under beds and around corners, just out of sight. Barely glimpsed, more smoke and mirrors, but present nonetheless. Some are visible, some not so much. Some shout me down in the dark, loud and raucous and dissonant. Some whisper in my ear, sibilant and soothing, urging me to wander paths best left untraveled. Fear keeps the lights on at night and smells of sweat and tension and anxiety - sharp and unpleasant. If the fear is great enough, it can keep me rooted and curled in on myself, covers pulled tightly over my head, unmoving. Paralyzed. Stuck. Tentative. Invisible.

But my faith: sweet and sure and graceful. It wraps around me like light, like breath, like life. It sometimes moves mountains. More often than not, it is just enough. Enough, not to beat back the darkness or vanquish the demons, but enough to put one foot in front of the other, to walk, however falteringly, forward. To know that, no matter what, I am enough, I will be ok.

And so, faith and grace being what they are, I think of my fear, and my *stuckness*, and I am reminded that it is *Pesach* (Passover). And in the midst of all of this darkness, there is also redemption, and release.

I got to tell the story of Nachshon at assembly a few Sundays ago at my synagogue. It is my favorite *midrash*, I think. Nachshon was a slave with all the other Israelites who found redemption at the hand of God. He was Let Go, with a capital L and a capital G, brought out with a Mighty Hand. He packed and didn't let the dough rise and ran, breathless and scared and grateful, away from the land of Pharaohs and pyramids and crocodiles and slavery - ran into freedom.

And then he got to the Sea. He and 600,000 other un-slaved people. Stopped cold by the Red Sea. It was huge, and liquid, and deep. You couldn't see the other side. It was so big you couldn't see *any* sides. Just wet, from here to... forever.

And behind him, when he (and 600,000 others) dared to peek: Pharaoh and his army of men and horses and chariots. And spears and swords and assorted sharp pointy things. We really can't forget the sharp pointy things. Even at a distance, the sharp pointy things loomed quite large in the eyes of Nachshon and his recently-freed brethren. Caught between the original rock and a hard place. Well, between water and pointy metal stuff. At this point, no one involved cared much about getting the metaphor exactly right. What they cared about was getting out from that perilous middle. Fast.

So Moses, because it was his job, went to have a chat with God. And just like that, Moses got an answer - a Divine Instant Message. All that the Children of Israel needed to do: walk forward, into the Sea, that big, wet, deep forever sea. God would provide a way. "Trust Me," God seemed to say. "I got you this far, didn't I? I wouldn't let you fall now!"

And Nachshon and the 600,000 stood at the shivery edge of that Sea, staring at that infinite horizon in front and the pointy, roiling chaos of death and slavery behind them. And they stood. Planted. And let's face it: not just planted, but rooted in their fear and mistrust and doubt. They may have felt reassured by the image of God as a pillar of smoke or fire - impressive pyrotechnics to be sure - but the soldiers and the Sea were so there, so present, so much more real.

And then, in the midst of that fear and doubt, something changed. Nachshon, lately freed, trapped between death by water and death by sharp, pointy things, did the miraculous: he put one foot in front of the other and walked into the sea. And the 600,000 held their collective breath, watching the scene unfold before them. Nachshon did what 600,000 could not (or would not; that may be another essay altogether): he decided to believe, to have faith. To leap. And though the water covered first his ankles, then knees, then chest, then kept rising, until he was almost swallowed whole, he kept walking, kept believing. And just when it seemed that Nachshon was a fool for his faith, would surely drown in that infinite forever sea, another miracle:

The waters parted.

The Sea split and Nachshon, so recently in over his head, walked on dry land. And the 600,000 breathed again, in one relieved whoosh of air, and they found their own faith and followed Nachshon into and across the dry Sea to the other side. And then their journey truly began.

I pray to have faith enough to walk into my own Sea - of doubt and fear and darkness. I want to walk and feel the waters part, to be released from the tangled web of thought that holds me immobile and disconnected. I have learned, again and again, without fail: when I take that step, when I find the grace and the faith to put one foot in front of the other, to trust, as Nachshon did, I am carried forward, I am freed from my self-imposed bondage. I am enough, and I can walk again on dry land to freedom.

Opening the Door

There is a moment during the N'eilah service on Yom Kippur that stays with me, always. I want to say that it haunts me, but that's really not the right image. It's more a flooding, a rushing-out-and- rushing-in-at-the- exact-same-moment kind of thing. It is the instant of my surrender - to the moment, to God, to being.

I love that moment. I stand and pray and sing and fast and ask and wait and thirst and hunger, all day long, again and again, in a ritual that takes me to the desert wilderness and back again. I stand at those gates, and finally, near the end, when I am cold and dry-mouthed and my skin is fairly buzzing with weariness, I give.

I give, and all the artifice, all the ritual, all the expectation goes out in a single breath of air and lightness, replaced in an instant with quiet surrender. I stand before the gates, ready to walk through, and know that as I do, I will be met by God. Neither in nor out, but exactly there, time flows again, and I step through.

A gate. A doorway. Redemption. I am transfixed by the notion of standing at the gates.

That said, it should come as no surprise that I am also caught by the doors of Passover. The first door is an invitation. "This is the bread of our affliction," we say. "Let all who are hungry come and eat. Let all who are needy come and celebrate the Passover." There's more, but this is the heart of it: open the door. The first time I read those words, I wept. The first time? Who am I kidding - every time I read those words, I weep. There is a world of hurt and need, just beyond our walls. Open the door and let others in.

The second door is Elijah's. As children, we waited so expectantly, so watchfully. Did the wine shiver and disappear - even a little? Did something brush against a cheek or bump a chair? Year after year, we opened the door, bowing to ritual, but mostly just welcoming in the fresh air, and almost-but-not-quite believing that this would be the year that Elijah would come - to visit, to herald, to usher in *Moshiach*. Even as children, did we really expect such a miracle? Do we now? But we open the door, to Elijah and the hope- or perhaps merely the thought- of redemption.

This year, as we have every other year, we opened the door during our Seder, first for those in need, and then later for our redemption. It was no different than any other year. Not really. Certainly, it was noisier (the best kind of noisy: kids and adults engaged, excited, participating, singing, talking, laughing, sometimes even praying). It felt more crowded and more relaxed and more wonderful than Seders I had experienced over the last handful or two of years. But not different. Not really.

We opened the doors. We recited the words. We closed the doors. And then we got on with it. It felt, if not different, then perfunctory and unfinished. Sitting in Shabbat morning services a week later, I was struck with this thought: how utterly un-Jewish those Passover doors are.

And there it was, the source of my unease, my dissatisfaction: *Since when do we, as Jews, require that those in need come to us for aid? Since when do we wait?*

We are not a people who sit idly by. We act. We do. We repair. And we do this, when we do it most Jewishly, joyfully, purposefully. We climb the ladder that Maimonides showed to us so that we can reach out to others - enable others - to become independent and productive. And always, always, we repair our world with compassion: no shame, no fanfare, no tickertape parades. To wait for those in need to come to us, to announce to us their need, seems to fly in the face of our teaching.

I am reminded of a story that was told to me a decade or two ago. A woman was talking to a friend, bemoaning the lack of relationship-worthy partners. Her friend thought for a moment and said "Write a list of all the qualities you want in a partner. When you're done, come back and we can talk." The woman went away, thoughtful. She worked diligently on her list; if it was to be her List (with a capital "L"), then she wanted it to be her List in the best of all possible worlds kind of list, covering all the bases and every contingency. At last she was done and she came back to her friend, handing it over somewhat triumphantly. She was quite proud of her list of qualities. The friend glanced at the list, nodding her head occasionally. In short order (too short, thought the List creator), she handed back it and said "Now, become all these things."

How Jewish! We climb that steep ladder of *tzedakah*, we practice the obligations of *tikun olam* (repair of the world), yes, because it is the right thing to do, but also because we do not wait. Do we want the Messiah to come? Then we must build a world in which the Messiah would like to be. To put it another way: we must become the change we want to see. We must act to build a better world.

Those doors of Passover - so filled with hope and potential! But it is not enough to just open the door and hope. It cannot be. There is no time to wait for those who hunger, or thirst, or need to come to us. We must step through those doors, into the world, to heal and repair, to be the change we want to see. We must step through the doors of Passover, and know that, as we do, there is God - there, exactly there. Perhaps it is there, exactly there, that we are redeemed.

The Holiness of Silence

I remember the silence of the desert.

I entered those wild lands
of heat and cracked earth
and wind that twisted
everything it kissed.

My shadow danced, a stumbling gait
on the solitary plains
and morphing hills that rose
and sank and shimmered
under a sky deserted of
clouds.

I felt its blueness.
It lay heavy on my skin,
and tasted of bronze,
burnished -
polished -
swept clean
And empty.

I saw visions there,
and felt the echoes of
stardust,
and still my shadow danced -
there was no hiding from it
in the silence and sere beauty
Of wind and earth and trackless glory.

I walked
And danced
And stumbled
Weary
In a vast and antique land
Of dangerous,
Of desolate grandeur,
To gather together
My brokenness,
To return to the gate of Heaven
And rest, at last,
In the hand of God.

I remember the desert,
And the holiness of silence.

Shavuot

What I Brought

I stood on the border of my wilderness.
It beckons in silent commandment,
My feet feeling for the road
That is dusty and half hidden
Under brambles and
Desire.

I am draped in cloth of gold
That pales under a sun of glory
Rings of silver and lapis
Grace my graceless fingers
And offer only a hollow echo
To the spark of stars and moonlight
That litter the night sky.
Laden with my gathered gifts

I gather in the best of me
My harvest
Reaped
To leave at the foot of Sinai
At the altars of God.
I traverse the desert
In forty nine steps
Spinning my measure of grain into
A promise

One day. And the next
And again
And yet again.
Days pass

I am gathered in
To leave at the altar
My best
For God.

I stand at the foot of that mountain
And I tremble
In wearied joy
And exultant fear.
I reach for my offering basket,
To lay it full upon that altar.
And see behind me
In that trackless
Silence
My fruit
My first and finest gifts
Tumbled and trampled
Stretching back forty nine steps and more -

And I weep.

I lay my tears on that altar
With my sorrow
And my yearning
My hopeless desire
My brokenness
And pain
For I have nothing left to offer
(That is mine to give)

And I turn to collect bright feathers.
They drift down around me,
A shower of white and gold, and silver and lapis
A glinting

Glistening opal fire
Of glory
And I gather them up
Gather them in
Fashioning them into wings
Of scattered light
And I fly.

An Absence of Color and Light

We sat among the willows,
and we wept,
there by the river
that flowed
clear and cold and swift,
 - branches dancing,
barely dancing -
as they swayed
and swept the ground.

We stood among the weeping trees,
Prayers mixed with
visions of ash.
and smoke
that rose and billowed,
Black against purple-stained blue
 - the blue of periwinkles
and royalty -
and a sky smudged with soot and
an absence of color
and Light,
and the altars we had left behind.

How can we sing
with no stone walls
adorned with lapis and gold:
 - the blue of royalty
and the blaze of the sun -
How,

before that pillar of fire,
that billowing smoke
that is empty of God
and absent of Light?
That raged in a fiery, metallic storm,
licking at loose rubble,
that once was strong walls,
that once was adorned with
the presence of God?

We wept,
and did not sing,
and found no music
in our unstrung lyres
and broken harps.
We wept,
for how could we sing?

And after the weeping
and the fire
and the absent,
Empty,
broken altars -
Pale morning.
and skies of purple-stained blue
shot through with scarlet and gold.
Mist tangled in those willows,
their branches dancing -
barely dancing -
barely skimming the swiftly flowing waters.

A moment -
A breathless,
silent

sacred moment.
that was a psalm,
A hymn of color,
and holiness
Made anew.
And there was no absence.
And there was light.

And there,
among the willows
by that swiftly flowing river,
We found a new prayer
And sang.

Rosh Hashanah

In the Space of *T'kiyah*

This is about the 19th iteration of my personal reflection. The 19th of today, and the 19th written down. There have been infinitely more than 19 iterations playing in my head, ever since I was so kindly asked me to write one for Rosh HaShanah. *Knowing* what I want to write has not been the issue. Getting it right, finding all the words and hearing the flow of it - that's been a bit of a challenge.

There are too many words, too many ideas and things to say, floating around in my head. I know, somewhere, somewhen, that they connect. I can feel that, feel them all jostling for position, taking up residence in some little known and cobwebbed corner of my head, leaving a faint pattern in the dust and clutter.

"Pick me!"

"Pick me!"

"Start here..."

Except, when I poke around, to find which of the eleventy-seven stories running around loose in my head is whispering "start here..." I get lost. That internal torch gutters, sending bizarre fun-house shadows to distort my visions, and then they all go skittering about, playing hide-and-seek with the shadows and light.

And so, since I can't find the beginning of this thread, can't seem to be able to tease and coax the end out from the tangled ball of string it has become, I thought about starting at the end. I could, but I don't know what that is yet either. So, I will pick one bright and shiny thing to start with, and see where that leads. It may be a beginning, though more likely, it will be a middle. There are many more middles than beginnings. I will pick one thing, and see what happens. I'm pretty sure I'll at least recognize the end, whenever we get to that.

So. First - redemption. It's all about redemption. *My* redemption, to be exact, and my quest for it. And my fear that I will never find it. Or receive it. And it's about God. It's all about God, too. Always. And my quest for God. And my fear that I will never find God or forgiveness. And that I will never be able to forgive God. The pain of this fear is almost unbearable.

I spent a couple of decades denying God and redemption both. That pain was unimaginable. I am reminded of the *midrash* of King David and the origins of the *Adonai S'fatai*, which is the prayer we say at the beginning of the *Amidah*. David, the rabbis tell us, had sent a man to his certain death for the sake of satisfying his own selfish need. The man, Uriah, was a man of honor. He would not be dissuaded when David had a sudden change of heart. He was killed in battle, along with most of his troops. David got word of Uriah's death just before evening prayers.

What was he to do? He knew that he would have to talk to God, to ask forgiveness. But - and here's the hard part - David's fear: what if God said no? What if God refused? David ran into the fields, running from himself, from his fear, from God, until he could run no farther. How could he ask God for forgiveness, when he couldn't forgive himself? He stopped, just as the setting sun hit the horizon, staining the sky with crimson and gold and purple, and he cried out, in his fear and longing "*Adonai s'fatai tiftach ufid yagid t'hilatecha...*"

God, open my lips, that I may declare your praise...

And with that prayer - filled to its very edges with pain and humility and hope and despair, David was forgiven.

Well sure, the voices in my head whisper, God can forgive *David*. Let's face it: he's, well, David. His very name means "beloved..." And you're not. You're... you. All bets are off.

It is my greatest longing, my unrequited quest - to be redeemed. To be forgiven. To dance in the palm of God's hand. To believe, if even for an instant, that though I may not be David, though I may not be Beloved, I may find a small piece of it, and that that may be enough.

Today is such a busy one! The Book of Life and Death is opened and the Gates of Justice swing wide. It's the birthday of the world. Today, we stand with awe and trepidation as we undertake the breathtaking majesty of diving inwards, a deep and long and solitary dive, into murky waters that make us gasp and shiver with cold. But eventually, the water warms and the silt and grit settle and we learn to see, to shine a light on the inside, all the beauty, all the pain, all the hope and need.

It is all about redemption.

Today is redemption and majesty and reflection and God. It is joy and celebration and hope and...

Whatever today is, whatever the ritual and tradition that surrounds this day may be, what today is, what today will ever and always be: my brother's *yahrzeit*. While my head hears whispers of "pick me" and "start here," my heart hears a steady murmur of "this is the second anniversary." And last year, for all the pomp and circumstance of Rosh Hashanah, for all my desperate yearning for redemption and God, drowning out the music and prayer and the triumphant sounding of the shofar that opened the Book and flung wide the Gate - all I could hear was the steady cadence of "This is the first anniversary of his death."

This is one of those days that I am less forgiving of God. This is the second thing.

I know - absolutely know - that God is not at fault in this. God didn't set the butterfly's wings to flapping that ended in the hurricane of my brother's death. There was no Divine Plan here. Randy smoked four packs of cigarettes a day, existed on caffeine and nicotine. He was diagnosed with stage four metastatic lung cancer when he was 45, and died when he was 47. Not a day goes by that I don't miss him, though I don't think of him every day like I did. Stretches of time go by - a handful of days, a week, some small length of time, and I will suddenly stop, feeling the ache of his loss like a stitch in my side, sharp and hot, receding into a dull throb until it is more memory than real. My breath doesn't quite catch in my throat when I think of him. Mostly. I say *kaddish* every Shabbat, and I do not weep. Mostly.

He died because he smoked. He died because he got cancer. But he died *today*, two years ago. On Rosh Hashanah, the day of pomp and circumstance and joy and celebration. I was with him in the hospital when he died, literally as the *shofar* sounded down the hall from his room, And so the Book was laid open and the Gates swung wide and my brother died, all in the space of *tekiyah*. And so today has suddenly become hard. And I am suddenly less forgiving of God.

And for all of that, when I stood in prayer and my knees began to buckle from the weight of my sorrow, when I was filled with an ocean of pain and loss, when I wanted to curse God - when I *did* curse God - there were hands that reached out to hold me steady, and strong arms to carry me through to firm ground. When I demanded of God, to God - where the hell are You? I was answered: here. No farther than the nearest heartbeat, in the still small voices of all those around me, who showed me, again and again, that I was not alone. Even in my pain, even in my doubt and despair, I was not alone.

And so, the third thing: Redemption.

I started there, I know. Perhaps my ball of string, with its jumble of tangled threads and hopeless mess, was less eleventy-seven different things and more a giant mobius strip of one. Perhaps it is all reflections and variations on a single strand. Perhaps, at least for me, it is all about redemption. And God. Ever and always.

I have spent a lifetime yearning for redemption. I have spent an eternity of lifetimes searching for God. I have declared my disbelief in God even as I feared that God didn't believe in me. I have shouted my rage and demanded answers and whispered my praise. And the thing I come back to, again and again, like a gift of impossible and breathless wonder -

It is not what I pray that matters. It is that I pray.

For all my yearning, for all my longing, what I don't ever realize is that I am redeemed. I have not been abandoned by God. Neither have I been forgotten. David had it right in his psalms: we cry out to God and we are healed. He didn't tell us "God only hears the pretty words." No: we find healing and redemption because *we cry out in our anger and our fear.*

I do not believe in a Santa Claus god, who bestows presents on the deserving: God does not provide parking spaces or jobs, nor do we win wars or sporting events as the result of our faith and prayers. Good people will die, evil people will prosper, the sun will continue to blaze in the noonday sky, world without end, *amen v'amen.*

In my faith, in my prayer, what I find, again and again - what I am given, again and again, is grace. What I get is strength and courage to face what life has placed in front of me in that moment...even if that thing is the death of my beloved brother. My faith is not a guarantee that I will never know fear, or that only good and happy things will happen. My faith, my prayer allows me to put one foot in front of the other and know that I will be carried through. And in that exact moment, the moment I take that step, I am enough and I am redeemed. And in that moment, I dance in the palm of God's hand.

Chanukah

War

I joke with my son: "I'm a pacifist with violent tendencies..."

He laughs. I laugh. And then I sigh - because sadly, it's true.

I remember talking to a gaggle of pre-teens once, telling them about my heroes, Dr. King and Gandhi. They wanted to know why, and I told them about non-violence. I climbed my metaphorical mountain and sat there, in some divinely serene lotus position, and the vantage point of my lovely, modern, suburban life, and waxed profound on the holy nature of peace. And one of the smart kids (being in 6th or 7th grade, they are all smarter than adults) raised his hand, and asked in a voice loaded with innocence, "But what about the Holocaust? Would you have fought then? If you could have killed Hitler, would you have?"

They all perked up then. They sensed blood. "I don't know," was my only answer. "I am really grateful I have never been in a position that I have to choose." Even as I said the words, I could feel my insides twist and churn. *Would I?* In those days, I was single and childless. Now - I have my beloved son. What if the threat were to him? Would I be able to maintain my position of non-violence if the threat were to my child rather than to me - or to my community?

Hannah had an answer. She lived with her seven sons somewhere in Judea. She supported Judah and the Maccabees, and worked to defeat Antiochus and his army. When the soldiers came, as they did to every Jewish household, to force conversion upon then, Hannah was so steadfast in her beliefs that she was able to watch those soldiers throw each of her seven sons off the roof of their house, one by one, because she would not kneel and pray to a false god.

What a bizarre twist on the Hillel story - he was stopped by a Roman soldier who put a sword to his throat and said "Teach me the Torah while standing on one foot. If you can, I will convert. If you cannot, I will kill you here." Hillel, we are told, thoughtfully stands upon one foot and answers, "That which is hateful to you, do not do to others. The rest is commentary. Now go study." And the general, so the story goes, did just that.

Hannah was told, "Bow down and pray or we will throw your sons to their deaths!" And she refused, because she was steeped in her faith. She held firm to her convictions and watched each of her sons die. Did they scream? Did she cry? Did the soldiers think twice, wondering how they could kill an innocent child? Did the soldiers question their inhumane orders? Did Hannah even once question a faith that could revere martyrdom over life? She was so sure that right was on her side; did she forget Moshe's cry: "Choose life!"

We were at war, fighting for our lives, our beliefs, our identity. And war - it changes you. It changes us all. We celebrate our victory over the Assyrians, and praise the bravery and might of Judah and Mattathias and the Maccabean army.

And still, I am torn, between my love for peace, my belief in nonviolence, my absolute conviction that violence only leads to violence, that it never solves anything. And I look around the world, at the wars and the conflicts that are killing us - all of us (because we are an "us," this world of ours, this human race of which we are a part) and I still cannot answer the question "Would you fight? Is there a Just War?" with more than an "I don't know, and thank God that I haven't had to make that choice."

It is Chanukah - a time to celebrate miracles and identity and victory. Perhaps - I hope, I pray - the lesson of this war, of any war, is not to help us answer the question "Would you fight?" but to spur us to redouble our efforts to create a world in which there is no war. Work for peace, for justice. Fight poverty and ignorance and need, not one another.

I am naive, I know. But that is my hope, even so, and I will cling to it, hold fast to it, work tirelessly for it.

Some time ago, war broke out in Gaza. It was horrific. People died. People lived in fear and anger and despair. I wrote this poem in response to the news, to express my own anguish over war and how it changes us all. I include it here, on this third night of Chanukah, because war is war, and I am a lover of peace...

And I am a Lover of Peace

War is not holy.
It is made of blood
and fed by fear,
Ravenous and insatiable,
It devours the world
In pieces.

It touches
Everything,
Ten thousand miles
Or five hundred feet
Or ten inches away.
It sends out
delicate, grasping, choking tendrils
to curl and
coil
over the rubble
of bombed-out buildings,
and the razor sharp ruin
of hearts and
Lives.

Blood is blood.
It seeps
red and
turns brown
and black
as it dries
in the dirt.
Yours.
Mine.
Theirs.

Blood is blood.

And the thing about war -
The madness
of its twisted,
tainted
suffocating existence,
Is that it changes
everything
it touches,
And it touches
everything,
So that a lover of peace,
who listens for God in the
stillness,
and finds God in small moments
of holy devotion,
And carries the music of God
Out into the world -

In war,
A lover of peace,
in a moment of quiet
Stillness,
Where once there was
God
to fill that holy space
of grace and glory,
And now there is only
Silence,
a lover of peace
Will learn to say:
Blood is blood,
But better their *blood than*

Ours.
And I am a lover of
Peace.

As if that matters.

War touches
everything,
And changes
everything,
And kills,
And shatters,
And destroys
What it touches.
And war is not holy
And war makes blood flow.

And blood is blood.
That matters -
Blood is blood,
And I am a lover of
Peace.

Bound to Freedom

Once we were slaves, now we are free.

That particular phrase, that particular concept is woven deep throughout my everything. Really. I am absolutely awed at the thought of such power and wonder and love (yes, love, because if I can anthropomorphize my relationship with God, I can certainly apply the same human logic and longing *to* my God).

One day we were slaves; the next - free. Ta da.

How does Chanukah fit in with all that? While we swap Moshe and his prophetic gravitas for Judah's guerrilla tactics and military prowess, the story remains hauntingly familiar: under the thumb of a king of great power who tried to break us, to take away our humanity, our spirit, our God, we were redeemed. And we have the miracles to prove it. Seas parted. Oil lasted. Food became a dicey prospect for digestive tracks. Fried food is merely a difference in degree, not kind, from matzo.

And after the redemption part? After the pyrotechnics and miracles and wonder and awe? Clean up on aisle seven...

Sure, we celebrate first. There's dancing and singing and praising galore!.I mean, really: we were redeemed! That is big - HUGE - awesome stuff! Talk about a *shehecheyanu* moment! Literally: thank you God, for bringing us to this season of joy. But what happens when that first blush of celebration is over? What happens when the music stops?

That's when the work of freedom really begins. Freedom is an action, not an event. It was never a gift; not for Moses and the people fleeing the narrow places. Not for Judah and the Maccabees and the other Judeans. There was a lot to attend to -nation building and temple-cleaning. Learning just what it meant to be God's people. This wasn't *freedom from* - or *freedom to* - . This was stay-in-the-game-freedom and do the work of being free. Because when you don't do that work, when you don't pay attention to the being free and being bound by that freedom, well, suddenly - you lose it. Suddenly, you're under a different thumb of a different king that is really just the same thumb of the same king, over and over again, ad infinitum.

And so tonight, on this first night of Chanukah, we gather to celebrate and find joy and sing praise (and eat latkes and spin dreidls and all that other family stuff of Chanukah-ing) - and we are reminded (I am reminded) that the work of freedom is part of the deal. Freedom binds me, to God, to you, to family, to the world, and so I find a purpose in it, and a fierce joy there. And with all that - the freedom and the binding and the joy - I celebrate the gift and grace of freedom.

Ribbons

The ribbon -
Now cut;
A neat snip of black cloth
On black cloth.
It disappears
Against a background of grief.

The ribbon -
Now cut;
It used to be torn.
Rent.
A whole tapestry,
A whole life.
Ripped and frayed,
Separate from itself.
No neat edges
Or symmetry,
No patchwork grace.
Just tangled threads,
Broken strands,
Dark on darker still,
Seasoned with salt and ash.

That ribbon of black -
Now cut;
Threaded through with light
That dances on hard edges
And skims along soft folds,
Offering a pale benediction,
And a sacred comfort,

A holy silence -
In a ribbon of black
Shot through with light
And cut -
Now cut,
Now broken
And frayed
And ragged-edged,
Woven in grief and praise.

Twenty Three

And so I will lay you down
In a field of gray grass,
Bending gracefully with the wind,
And shadowing a hidden, twisted path
That leads nowhere -
Or everywhere.
Back,
Forever back,
Until I stand again
At this place -
This field of fearful beauty.

I will lay you down,
Aching with weariness,
A hungering desire for
Your touch,
Your light,
Your laugh -
That is incandescent and
Pure,
And restores me -
And comforts me -
And feeds my soul.

I will lay you down
And weep,
And be made holy,
Sipping from a cup
That overflows with my grief.
But I will lay you down
And I will dwell forever
Sheltered only by the memory of you.

Mindfulness

The Arrow of Faith

We are commanded to attach fringes to our garments, along with a thread of blue, to remind us, ever and always, that I was bound and I am free, that I am commanded and holy. It is a difficult task, for me, to be this mindful, all the time. How awesome, that I have been given prompts to carry me through the year, arrows to my faith.

Knotted threads,
Gathered at the edges
and seen from the corners -
Suggestions only.
A wilderness of loosely
tangled, tattered strands,
all dancing,
dancing in supple
silken rhythm:
A single thread,
a hint of blue,
Reminds me -
Binds me -
Sets me free.

Be

I had a friend who used to say to me, "Stacey, you're a human being, not a human doing."

Ugh.

I am not overly fond of trite aphorisms (except insofar as they allow me to use words like "aphorism"). The problem with silly little phrases like this is that they tend to hold a kernel of truth, and belie a richness and depth that I can't really afford to ignore.

Here's the thing: I spend an awful lot of time doing. *Doing* is important. Holy, even. It is what allows us to accomplish, to move the needle and fix the broken stuff. To do is to put my faith in action, to crawl outside of my head and leave my tiny universe of one. To do is to connect, in some way, with the world around me and the people who inhabit it.

Like I said: holy.

Here's the problem, though: a lot of my doing is empty doing. It is motion for the sake of motion: frenzied, manic, shoot from the hip. I tend to be a whirling dervish of doing. I am the master juggler, tossing balls and oranges and chainsaws with equal aplomb. I am so intent on keeping everything from crashing to the ground, I don't ever stop to think why I'm running around with spinning plates to begin with.

Being is as holy as *doing*. It's part of the same sacred dance, a recognition that I am, that God is. It's a way to honor that *you* are. I don't need to define it any further. There is no modifier necessary, although I can certainly think of an infinite array of words - and each one of them, no matter how right, how fitting, how loving, each one limits and defines and boxes up the you or the me or the God, and in so doing, keeps us safe and disconnected and in control.

So, today, I am reminded that even amid the noise and chatter and constant motion of my life, even in purposeful doing, there is holiness in my stillness, in my simply being.

I am.

You are.

God is.

We are.

A holy declension of "to be," a sacred grammar.

Believe

I set out to write something profound here, some lyrical piece of prose that weaves a myriad of disparate threads into a single and vibrant whole that creates a luminous and holy path to Belief.

I want to bring you to the mountaintop, so that you can feel the presence of God, find that transcendent arc that allows you to dance in God's hand. I want to hear that sigh, of relief, of recognition - *yes; this is it, this is what I believe, this is good.* Like coming home after a hard journey, not to fanfare and parades, but to warmth and love and gentleness.

What I get, more often than not, is a heavy use of my delete key: pixels scattering through the ether, getting eaten by the very hungry ghosts in my machine. What I get, more often than not, is doubt.

Belief can be hard.

It feels so much like walking on a high wire without a net, belief does. It's a precarious perch, and I hate to admit that, after decades of mindful searching, I find I misplace my belief almost as often as I find it. Dammit - why can't I have what Maimonides proclaimed: *I believe with perfect faith...*

What I have learned - slowly, *very* slowly - is that my belief is a living thing: it grows and recedes and changes. What I believed as a child has changed. Thank God. Back then, I believed some pretty weird things, not least of which was that magic was real, unicorns lived and my baby brother was part chicken because he had to live in an incubator for a while after he was born (long story short: he was *not* part chicken, though he was jaundiced). As an adult, I can ask: What belief *hasn't* changed?

There was a time I did not believe in God.

There was a much longer (and more desperate) time I believed God didn't believe in me.

There was a time that I didn't believe in myself. This one is still true. Sometimes.

There was a time I believed I was broken, unfixable, irredeemable. That's the thing about belief: it changes. It deepens, softens, drifts in an ever-shifting pattern.

As I prepare to dance that transcendent and holy arc of the High Holy Days, I pause for a breath of time to challenge my beliefs, to be mindful of them, to examine them in the light of day and under cover of star-bright skies. When I look close enough, I can see, woven among the thousand, thousand strands of my belief, doubt and cynicism and naiveté. My disbelief is there to be challenged just as well.

Finally, I understand: It's all good - my belief, my doubt. It is neither black nor white, the world of my belief: it is a bright and shining place of glorious silver. I don't need to be like the Rambam; I don't need to believe *perfectly*, I just need to believe.

Bless

Sometimes, I'm convinced that I am cursed. Sometimes, I'm absolutely certain that my Higher Power, whom I mostly call God, but occasionally call something more suitable for an R-18 rated essay - I am certain that S/He is, in actuality, God's evil twin, and S/He is definitely out to get me.

I know this because life can be really crappy. Not just the every day crappy of traffic jams and paper cuts. I'm talking the huge, almost insurmountable crappy that can seep into all the cracks of your life, spreading over everything, until it's just ooze, from here to infinity plus three. It's all that big stuff that tears you apart, fills you with shame, tastes like despair. And after two or three or six times you realize that the bottom you swore you had finally landed on turns out to be just another trap door - all of that *crap* seems to wrap around you like cotton, muffling all the sounds, and blurring all the light.

Hard to see blessings through all that cotton batting and those loose trap doors.

So I curse, from the depths of whatever sub-basement of the six kinds of hell into which I've fallen. And into that echo-y, empty space that contains no light and holds less hope, I cry and mumble and dream and yell (depending upon the day, or the phases of the moon, or just how depressed/angry/ scared I really am) a string of invective that could blister ice. I swear - really, *really* swear. And I curse. A helluva lot.

There's not a blessing to be found.

This is what I tell myself: I must be cursed, and since this must be true, I only have curses to give. And I give them all to God. *That's* what fills this basket I carry with me - my anger. My pain. My despair. All the broken bits and open wounds. I carry it all with me, cursing God, cursing me, over and over, again and again.

But at some point in my twisty, winding, stumbling life, I learned this one holy thing: this, too, shall pass.

It is a holy thing. Trite to be sure, but no less a holy statement for all of that. **This will pass.** I know this, I have experienced is time and again, yet I wrap myself in that cotton, I slog through that desert of ooze that sucks at my feet and swallows my shoes, I curse and I moan and feel lost in forever. And I am surprised, still (always), that it does. There are times when I have no idea *why* it passes, just that one day, I felt buried by a mound of fifty-seven things that I couldn't climb on a good day with every superhuman power anyone could ever think of, and the next I wasn't.

Don't get me wrong. The crappy stuff, from tiny and stupid and annoying to the huge stuff that crushes your spirit and sips at your soul - all that crappy stuff is still there. The job is still lost. The bills are still stacked and overdue. People you love still die. Life is still hard.

What changes though, is not the *stuff*. What changes is *you*. Perhaps it's all the cursing. I am convinced that it doesn't ever matter what you pray, only that you pray. It is my continuing conversation with God - whatever God's name I call Her/Him, whatever mask I demand God wear - that makes a difference and changes me.

I don't know the mechanism for this change, or the equation that solves for X, where X is my pain, traveling along the Y-axis of my doubt divided by time and intention. I have no clue, and I am, much to my surprise, okay with that. I am learning to let be, let go, breathe. And you know what? That, too - that enlightened, spiritually wonky place of serenity and being-ness - that, too will pass. No matter how tightly I hold on, they pass.

Here's what I do know - when I stumble, when I stagger under the weight of my despair, there have been people who have caught me and carried me until I found firmer ground to stand on. There have been hands to hold in the darkness, shoulders upon which to lean and hearts to shine a light on hidden paths. I have been offered kindness, I have felt love. I have seen my son smile and heard him laugh as if pain had never been invented.

I may carry my curses with me, lugging them along as I trudge from place to place. But I carry my blessings, too.

I am blessed beyond imaging.

Clean

Growing up, my mother and I would reenact the same ritual every Tuesday and Thursday morning:

Mom: *Stacey. Go clean your room. Ann* [our housekeeper] *is coming.*

Me: Silence. Incomprehension. Clean my room before the housekeeper could do it for me? What? You cannot be serious! (All this totally inside my own head. I never bothered to respond out loud, as the suggestion was so ludicrous.)

And every Tuesday and Thursday morning, I would look around the mess of my room, go to school, and come back to a room that was clean - bed made, clothes hung or folded, depending, things dusted. It would smell of Pine Sol and bleach. I think. At least, those are the smells I associated with Ann's days at our house. This went on for years and years. It never changed: I'd make a mess; Ann would clean it up.

When I moved into my first apartment, I called my mother: "Ok, mom," I said, "I have a toilet bowl brush and it didn't come with instructions. How does it work?" She must have laughed a good five minutes. Sadly, she was with a group of her friends, playing bridge when I called. They laughed as long and as loud as mom.

"But you never taught me! When did I ever have to clean a toilet?" I didn't come close to understanding her amusement. I just thought my embarrassment was all her fault. Of course, at eighteen, what wouldn't have been my mother's fault?

I am no longer eighteen. Thank God. I can't imagine ever being that young, that innocent and naive and world-weary, all at the same time. I have since learned a lot about cleaning: I make my own bed most mornings. Do the dishes. Dust occasionally. Pick up after my son (and say "Clean your room; Mariola is coming today."). While cleaning the house is not on the list of the top 1,000 things I'd like to do, I do it anyway, because it needs to be done.

My house: mostly clean. If not scrubbed and shiny, then not embarrassing. If company dropped by unexpectedly, I would be able to invite them in. This was not always the case. There have been days (weeks) (I'm pretty sure not months, but who's counting?) where the mess was barely contained within the confines of my home. Sometimes, not contained at all. Was I the only one with a "magic closet," that could just as easily turn into a "magic bedroom?" While the "public rooms" of the house were neat(ish), the closet/bedroom was more of a war-ravaged mess or a pillager's treasure trove, depending upon your perspective.

And I knew, without a doubt, that my life and my mess were connected. The more chaotic my life, the more it went spinning out of control, the more chaos at home. I prided myself, at times, that at least I could find a place to sit for me and a friend or two. That I couldn't open certain doors was a secret I thought I'd carry to the grave. (So much for secrets.)

The prompt for today is "Clean." I love that there is no further direction or instruction. I started this essay thinking I would write about the cleaning necessary for Passover - the cabinets and dishes and pantries - transformed, shifted, cleaned. But I cannot write about what I don't do. And I do not clean for *Pesach*. I think about it. I flirt with the idea of keeping *kosher l'pesach* - as much as I flirt with the idea of keeping kosher. Period.

They are interesting, lovely thoughts. They are rife with spiritual nuance. I don't do 'em. As for why - that is fodder for another essay altogether. Maybe. Maybe I'll even do it this year - the kosher for *Pesach* thing, the cleaning and scrubbing and transforming thing, and I will (I'm sure) (and I say that with no cynicism or sarcasm whatsoever; I really *am* sure) find something rich and meaningful and holy in those actions.

But remember - no direction, other than that the prompt is "Clean." So I go where I always go, in these cases, which is where I want to go: cleaning my mental and spiritual house. Cleaning my insides, scrubbing and polishing and transforming and renewing, all the inside stuff. That is part of this journey, just as much as switching dishes and removing *chametz* from my house.

There is something incredibly powerful in diving a little deeper, shining the light a little brighter, coming clean - really clean. Know thyself - but not just *know*. Know yourself so well that you can forgive yourself your humanity, unlock the chains that keep you tethered and enslaved - the pain and the grief and the shame, ask forgiveness of those you've harmed, and strive to do it differently, do it better, do it right as you put one foot in front of the other.

And when I can do this - clean the house of my spirit - there is such light, such joy! Once we were slaves; now we are free.

Count

I count everything; it is a small, and I hope harmless, obsession.

I count words. I have to, as a writer, especially considering that my personal motto seems to be "why use ten words when a hundred will do?" It is more granular now, counting not words but characters in a text, though they keep changing the rules and I have no idea how many characters are allowed in text. My son thinks me very unhip for not knowing.

I count steps - both the move-yourself-forward-from-one-place-to-another as well as the move-yourself-up-and-down-in-a-building. There are fourteen steps to a floor in my building. There are 1,500 between me and the nearest Starbucks.

I use six grape tomatoes in my salad, cut in half. Always. If there are olives, there are five.

I count calories, points and carbs in some complicated kabbalistic iteration. I am not as obsessed with this as I should be, as the pounds on my scale will attest. I count pills out and calculate how many ccs of insulin I need to take. I am much more religious about counting these out, and I resent every one of them.

I have 852 friends on Facebook and 28,732 people have viewed my blog. I am not particularly proud that I know these things, but I do, nonetheless. Just checked - make that 28,797 views. And since I was checking, I have 87 drafts and 193 published posts there. I counted once, about 4 months ago; there were about 80,000 words then. I'm guessing (and yes, I'm sure I'll check after I've done writing this) there are another 10,000 words since. Maybe more.

It has been 8,066 days since my last drink. Twenty-two years and a month, exactly. I could do the hours and minutes, but that's not an accurate picture. In the early days of my sobriety, time didn't function well. There were a few passes through eternity then. And even now, every once in a while, there are minutes, or hours or days that seem to stretch well beyond the borders they are supposed to measure.

Three years, eleven months and 30 days ago my brother died. I would give anything to stop counting those days. Or rather, to have no reason to count them. Thing is, 1,460 days is just a way station. Tomorrow the count will be one more than that, and one more the next day, and on and on. It is a meaningless, impossibly difficult calculus. Tomorrow will be his Americanized *yahrzeit*. I will mark it. I will remember and perhaps cry. And I will relive it, this sadness and mindful remembrance, in a few weeks - in eighteen days, to be exact, for his Hebrew *yahrzeit*. Lucky me.

I count, and I measure, and I count again. I add time and things and steps - as if any of this mattered. As I walk through this month of Elul, and dive a little deeper, bend the light around me differently, live my days more mindfully - none of that counting matters. For me, it is an attempt, sometimes clever, sometimes manic, but always, always, always - it is my attempt to control my life. It is not a calculus of grief, nor am I solving for X. My counting is so much more hopeless: a magical incantation to make all of the disparate and desperate strands of my life fit neatly on the little boxes I have labeled for them.

I cannot control all of those pieces. I can't. I have learned that lesson again and again. Life - and death - are what they are: a perfect tautology. Where I find peace, where I find that place of comfort and I fit inside my own skin - it is when I *stop* counting, when I stop focusing on all of the things that measure, and let my life - and all of the swirling pieces that fill it so fully - just come. Just flow. I am not here to measure my life. I am here, with all the grace I can muster, to live it.

Dare

On my one year sober anniversary, I felt somewhat at a loss. I mean, really - how in the world do you celebrate *anything*, if not with a flute or seven of champagne (merely as a prelude to the serious drinking that was sure to follow)? I went to my regular meeting and announced for all the world to hear (or at least the 27 people who were present): *I have one year, today.*

I'd seen the drill a thousand times. OK, maybe not a thousand, but at least one or two at every meeting I went to (which was pretty much a daily occurrence), someone announced his or her anniversary. Some counted days. Some, months. There were many of these folks at every meeting. For some, it took months, sometimes years, to put some time together. Often, we'd hear "I have 3 days. Again" or "I'm back. Got two weeks this time." Some iteration of time and desperation and hope.

Incremental anniversaries were announced, but there were always a helluva lot fewer people making these announcements as the years went up. Two years. Three. Seven. Seventeen. With each bigger chunk of time, the number of people to reach those milestones became fewer. One year anniversaries were kinda special. At the one year mark, it was as if you had crossed a magic line - you'd made it, member of the club. Not that it would be a slam-dunk guarantee of sobriety, forever and ever, world without end, amen. Not that (not ever that). But at a year, there was a recognition that, at the very least, there was a chance that sobriety just might stick.

So I announced my anniversary. I felt a little proud; I felt a little lost. There was applause and exclamatory congratulations flew across the room. I got the obligatory "How'd ya do it?" followed quickly with my equally obligatory "With the help of God and the fellowship of this program!" It was a script we'd all played at before, in one role or another. Right at that moment, I didn't believe a word of any of it.

Frankly, I had no idea how the hell I'd stayed sober for a year.

We went for coffee and to grab a bite after the meeting. No champagne. I got a chip - a brass coin - embossed with a giant Roman numeral I on one side, and "To thine own self be true" on the other. I got a rose. And I got a card. The front was kinda sappy - watercolor flowers and "Hooray! Hooray!" Lots of exclamation points. Or at least, it felt like a lot. I opened it.

This was another of those truth things, found unexpectedly. It hit me between the eyes and took my breath away. Hooray, hooray -

"You did the thing you feared the most!"

And I realized, in that instant, that I had. Sobriety was a terrifying prospect when I was just starting. How in the world can you live without a drink to calm you and protect you and put a glassy, fluid shield between you and the rest of the universe? How in the world do you face life raw and vulnerable? How in the world can anyone dare to hope - that things will change, that life gets better, that there is forgiveness and perhaps even love?

How? A day at a time. A day at a time, a minute, an hour, a breath - you do the thing you fear the most.

In honor of that long ago moment, that changed my life and opened my heart: for today, for this moment, I will dare to live a life of hope. I will dare to trust, and pray, and believe. For today, I will let faith overrule my fear. For this moment, I will brave the shadows. For today, I will reach out to offer strength and kindness, to shine a light in your darkness.

For today, for this moment, in this breath - this eternal and infinite breath - I will do the thing I fear the most, and I will dare to leap...

End

I just finished an essay for the prompt "End." Literally just entered the last period, formatted the text, did the spell check. Every word of it was true. Every word was insanely false, a discordant klaxon of wrongness that made my teeth and my fingers clench. I have enough tension happening these days; I really don't need another source.

So. I'm scrapping that first essay, that was true, but that rang false.

End.

Here's the honest and true thing about End to me. *Nothing ends.* At least, nothing in *my* life does. Mainly because I won't let it.

I live in a land of never-ending forever. I don't let things end - not relationships, not friendships, not bad situations. And the good stuff - the happy, the fine, the soft and gentle and kind stuff? I cling to that with a death grip. I hold on so tightly that my nails dig into my palms a little too deep, and I break the thing I was trying to hold

Sad will never end.

Pain will never end.

Happy will never end - as long as I can control it, make it stay, make it last.

Because, when things end, when I let them go, wherever it is that they go to when they do go, when I let them, then all I am is *alone*. And *that* really, really never ends.

Every word here rings true. Sings it, in some minor key that is so fragile and tragic and makes my heart hurt. Every word rings true, and it is all false. Every word.

I cannot allow myself to stop at the first turn, the first tug of resistance, to end before I really dig deep. Because the second and the third and the fifteenth - every turn after this first one has shown me that things end - marriages, friendships, happily-ever-after, and dark and stormy nights - they all end, and sometimes I'm alone, and sometimes I'm not. But even the aloneness ends.

Keep the gates open, God! Please - open the gates so that I may step through, to find You, and redemption. We say this, again and again. Keep the gates open. I forget that I have my own gates. I forget that, in my fear, in my joy, how easily I close them, lock them up tight. I close myself off to everyone and everything, and I am, indeed, alone. Perhaps physically, although, let's be honest - so what? That's just a momentary thing.

When I remember, when I choose, when I do the work, I keep my own gates thrown open, and when I do, all of my aloneness ends.

Enslave

This is the story of the last time I drank.

Now, this isn't a dramatic blowout of a drinking story. I don't even know that I got drunk. Maybe I was drunk-ish; you know, that kind of blurry feeling of lightness, as if you're on the Tilt-o-Whirl on a hot summer day, and you can't keep from spinning (and you don't want to), and you can't keep from smiling that big fun-house grin, and you're almost but not quite coordinated, and oh! You feel grand. Dizzy but grand.

It was that kind of a drunk.

It was my favorite kind of drunk. It was the drunk to which I aspired every time I got drunk. I had a lot of practice flirting with that razor-thin line. I failed in this particular endeavor. Often.

Those days, it seemed as if I failed at this a lot.

It hadn't always been an exercise in failure. It hadn't always been a constant internal battle for white-knuckled control. I had an elaborate set of rules and dicta regarding my drinking, to ensure victory over my drunks. That the first dictum was "I don't drink" will give you an idea of just how successful I was.

I used that particular argument all too often - I don't drink... so therefore, this particular drunk is an anomaly, an exception. It doesn't count in the long line of drunks that stretched back way too long ago and far away for me to count. I would remind myself that logical proof didn't depend on truth, but on soundness. The argument was bent, perhaps, but it was sound.

Life started to become unmanageable. Untenable. I started searching for a way out. I started pointing fingers, looking to lay blame on anyone or anything that wasn't me. It was my parents. My family. My past. My pain. Everything would be ok if everyone would just do what I wanted them to. Needed them to.

I flirted with several Twelve Step programs - none of them AA. I flirted with all their subtly different versions of the Steps. Well, I flirted with the first two of the twelve. I got the powerlessness of the first, mostly understood the God vs. Craziness of the second. And was stopped short by the third: Turned our will and our lives over to the care of God as we understood Him. And so I commenced the Twelve Step two-step, bouncing between one and two again and again, flailing and failing at three.

And drinking. And more and more unable to not drink, even when I swore I didn't and swore I wouldn't.

So. The last time. It was August in Chicago, a dark and humid and breezy night. And humid. Did I say humid already? I'll say it again, times six. Remember - Chicago in August. The night was dense and the air almost liquid. I was helping a friend move into a third floor walk-up apartment. It was a great place - old world, with lots of wood and built-ins and molding. And no air conditioning. Not even a window unit. We ended around 10:00, sweaty and sore.

"Want a beer?" He called out from the kitchen. I was in the living room, all the windows open, the curtains billowing madly. I could barely move. A beer. I don't drink.

"Sure." I don't drink.

He handed me a bottle, slick with condensation. I took the offered beer (and I remember the weight of it in my hand, the cold of it still), sitting back on the broken-springed couch, and I thought to myself "If I take this, if I drink it, I will be turning my will and my life over to the care of alcohol."

And all the struggle, all the doubt, all the fight left me in a whoosh, and I drank, deep and long. Not only was I ok with that pronouncement, I was sure that I was finally in the place I was always meant to be.

Enslaved, bound to my demons with liquid fire.

And the next day, bleary and hung over and done, another friend, a different friend, loved me enough to tell me "Drink, don't drink, that's up to you - but you're an alcoholic!" And with those words, I was suddenly freed. I stood on the borders of my own desert, at the edge of a distant and implacable sea, and found, much to my surprise, some internal sense of permission to get help, and so find forgiveness and grace.

I know, one of those immutable truths that I hold in my very center, that miracles abound, that there is redemption, that once we were slaves and now we are free.

Fear

Fear is a liar.

Fear keeps me rooted in place, unmoving and sheathed in ice. When I listen to its sibilant whispers, I stop. I hide. I avoid. I stay safe.

It is so easy. looking at it from this vantage point - of a spiritually fit place, where I feel as if I fit comfortably in my own skin and have no need to look over my shoulder to judge the distance between me and the eleventy-seven thousand demons who are hot on my trail and ready to pounce - it is so easy to say "Fear is a liar. Why should I listen to whispers in the dark?"

Trouble is, I don't always feel comfortable in my own skin. I am not always spiritually fit, confident and breathing easy. Ha! There are times I need to be reminded to breathe at all. And fear - those lies can be so seductive. When I am feeling prickly and outside and less-than, those lies can flow though me and around me like warm honey.

Remember Lucy asking Charlie Brown to kick the football while she holds it steady? Time and again, he winds up flat on his back, caught once again in the web of Lucy's broken promises. My fear is like that. Against my better judgment, regardless of all prior experience, I get sucked in, laid low by my fear.

This is not God-fear. This is not the fear and trembling of standing under Sinai or waiting at the cold and dark waters of an unparted Sea. This is not the fear and awe of standing at the gates of return and redemption. This is the fear that robs you of hope, breaks your spirit and keeps you rooted: stuck, unmoving, trapped.

I have heard that fear is the opposite of faith, that if I have faith enough, I will never be afraid. I don't agree. Faith and fear can coexist. Here's the thing of it: my faith will not stop my fears, will not stop the whispered lies - but enough faith will keep me moving. I don't know that faith can move mountains; I know for a fact that faith can move my feet, allow me to put one foot in front of the other, walk through the fear, so that I can get to the other side, face whatever is in front of me. Every time.

As I prepare to stand before God in a few days (that formal stand-before-God, because I believe, absolutely, that I stand with God, always, just as God stands with me, always), as I prepare to stand without artifice or design, ready to walk through the gates that are opened for us all, I have to be willing to leave the things that hold me back, hold me in place, behind. I have to be willing to leave the fear that feels so safe and comfortable, because it is so familiar, because it is so powerful and all-encompassing; I have to leave the fear behind.

I have to let it go, along with my brokenness, my cynicism, my impatience. I have to be willing to walk away from Lucy and her football and not play the game.

I have to put one foot in front of the other. And later, and again, when fear grips me, when I feel broken and lost and utterly alone, when fear whispers its lies to me in the dark - I will put my faith in my feet and keep walking.

Forgive

I have been writing a series of essays that I call *The Enough Essays*. I started the project a while back, as the result of a chance meeting, an act of supreme bravery, and a sudden realization that, in fact, I am - in and of myself - *enough*.

That first piece is mostly about the generalities of my enoughness. As I was polishing it and putting on the finishing touches, I had a small epiphany: I realized that I am enough in a whole *bunch* of ways. This is not to say that I'm perfect in any of them - not by a long shot! But I'm also not woefully deficient. So adding to the general *enoughness*, I wrote about them as well: faith, hope, grace, world-saving and mom-hood. They're scattered throughout my blog, in no particular order, though most have the word "enough" in the title.

There are more - some posted on my blog, many more still swirling about in my head, waiting to be written. There are always more, because one of the gifts of diving deep and discovering who I am and how I fit, is finding all those pieces of enoughness.

But here's the thing, the secret thing, the *I'd-really-like-to-keep-this-under-a-rock* thing: there are some dark places in there. Places I'd prefer not to disturb. Places I'd have to use a ladder to get to far-from-being-enough. I won't bore you with the gory details. If that means the hidden spots stay hidden a little while longer, so be it. They've managed to thrive as they lurk and slither through the muck.

I want to dive a little deeper, shine the light a little brighter. As scary as those dark and twisty places are, there are a few questions that I can't quite keep quiet. Not now, not while I've committed to walking this particular path. So.

When am I forgiven enough - for my humanity, my brokenness? When do I say I've had enough pain? When do I demand "Enough" and then have the courage to lay all those broken bits of me, the hidden places and twisted secrets - when do I have courage enough to lay them down? How can I be redeemed when I still cling to all of this, more intimately than a lover's embrace?

How can I ask your forgiveness, ask forgiveness of God, when I cannot forgive myself?

And perhaps *because* I strive to be mindful, because I have committed to illuminating all of me - the good, the bad, warts and all - I am reminded (when I get quiet enough, am still enough): when I leap, I am caught. Without fail. I know how to forgive, how to show up with compassion and kindness. For you. Perhaps I need to dive a little deeper, and find the compassion of forgiveness for myself.

And those leaps? They don't have to be made with seven mile boots. A stumble, a step at a time is enough. Who knows - maybe this is the year I will find forgiveness enough to return.

Hope

I knew I would love The John Laroquette show from the very first episode: a cynical, sarcastic, self-deprecating, trying-to-get/stay-sober alcoholic who had bottomed out after losing everything and was desperately trying to piece his life back together without getting too attached to it, without allowing himself to care too much about it.

Not that I identified in any way to this character setting. Not that I appreciated the gallows humor a little too well. At all. Actually, what drew me in, what made me exhale in easy recognition was a sign that hung on the wall of John's office:

This is a dark ride.

Five words that captured my life, framed everything, in perfect context. You must know (by now) that one of my mottoes is "Why use ten words when a hundred will do?" But there, hanging on the (fake) wall of the (fake) bus station's (fake) night manager's (fake) office was this five-word sign. A sign of absolute and immutable truth: this is a dark ride.

Angels could have sung in twenty-seven part harmony, while demons and dybbuks danced a tarantella and God tossed confetti on the lot of them. My Truth, writ in fake Gothic font on signboard and hung in all its pixellated glory, on the walls of a set for a TV show.

Life before hope. Life, when hope was a dirty little secret, an impotent exercise in futility and failure. Pandora would have been better served had she shut the box lid on Hope's tiny gossamer fairy wings when she had the chance.

And, okay, maybe not life without hope. More life with a hope that was misplaced and passive. I hoped for all the wrong things - that you would save me, that God would heal me, that life would magically work in my favor. That I would be happy. It's not that these were *bad* hopes. It's how I went about hoping.

What I did was exactly *nothing*. I did not ask, nor pray, nor act, nor choose. I sent my hope out into the universe (my tiny universe of one, that shut out light and air and the voice of God), whispered and weightless, and I waited. I waited to be struck whole. I waited to be made happy. I waited to be saved from myself. With every whispered prayer for hope I released, I got sadder and angrier and more self-righteously justified in my pain and loneliness.

What I didn't understand - what took me halfway to forever to learn - was that hope is an action. I am responsible and obligated to participate in my redemption. You will never save me. You can offer me strength and shine a light on my path - you can even lend me some hope. But you will not save me. You will not make me happy. You don't have that power (of course, it also means you cannot make me sad, or angry). Those are all inside jobs.

God will not strike me whole, heal my brokenness, relieve me of my despair. I won't even get into the circular and didactic argument of "Well, God could if S/He wanted..." That's not the point, not in my belief set. I can dance in the palm of God's hand, and find respite and release (and I have). My faith and my prayers change me, give me grace to walk forward in my life, face whatever is in front of me - the good stuff and the bad.

Pray to God, but row towards shore. Hope is an action. I have to hope with my feet. If I merely watch from the sidelines of my life, waiting for hope to kick in, life will be an eternally dark ride. Hope, as an action, as a prayer, lifts me and fills me and allows me not just to leap, but to soar.

Justice

Sometimes, Justice is a sword, slicing cleanly through anything that stands before it. I have walked into its cutting blade, and I have not been unscathed.

Sometimes, Justice is a mighty river, rushing through in a grand sweep, cold and pure, washing us clean and bringing about change. I have swum in its quickening current, slaked my thirst in its icy depths, been carried and cleansed and renewed.

We pursue it, always: *Justice, justice shall you pursue*. So central to our beliefs, it was named twice. We are called to it, commanded to practice it. It is the foundation of who we are as a people. A few months ago, during our *tikun leyl Shavuot* (our study session to usher in Shavuot), I had one of those Aha! moments that change us, even just a little. One of my greatest joys in Judaism is my continued struggle with it. I wrestle with God and Torah and my doubt. I have severe issues with our ancestors (the original Family Dysfunction, writ large). Don't get me started on God - so often seemingly capricious and cruel and uncaring.

And yet, I have this thing with God. I have met the God of Infinite Compassion. I have danced in the palm of God's hand, and found shelter there. I have wept and cursed and prayed to God, and have found healing there.

But this is not the God of the Torah. Sorry. I just don't see it. So what keeps me coming back to this well, this gate, again and again? How do I navigate this disconnect?

On Shavuot, we had a discussion on our relationship with God and Torah. And it came to me, in a rush, and filled me - the beauty of Torah (and yes, I believe it, we, all of life *is* Torah) is that we have been given all of it - *all* the holes, *all* the inconsistencies, *all* the brokenness. But we also get those moments of shining transcendence, those take-your-breath-away pieces that show you not what is, but what could be, what should be. We are commanded to create a world that *should* be. This is a holy thing.

This is the God of Justice, and we are *b'tzelem elohim* - we are made in the image of God. This is what we could be. This is the God I seek. This is the

God to whom I return, again and again. This is the God who redeems and renews.

God may be the One who changes me. I am the one who is given the holy task of changing the world. My Aha! moment. The reason I have sought to reflect and prepare, make the long and bumpy journey from my narrow places to the center, to this gate, to this day. Why I seek God and forgiveness. To return, to be redeemed, so I can step through the gates of Justice and change the world.

One more story, because I love it. A short *midrash* for Yom Kippur:

An old man, stooped with age, made his way to his synagogue on erev Yom Kippur. One of his greatest joys was to hear the simple yearning, the exquisite longing in *Kol Nidre*, the prayer that begins it all. He couldn't remember a time that he did not weep when he heard it, not once, but three times, every year. He walked slowly, enjoying the just-beginning-to-cool, almost-fall air. One hand held his cane that tapped and scraped against the sidewalk. The other hand cradled two heavy notebooks.

He entered the synagogue, which smelled of lemon oil and anticipation. He paused to offer a prayer as he put on his white *tallit*. He stopped at the memorial wall and remembered friends and family who had died. Each year, there were more, and he let his grief and sorrow flow through him, letting it go with love and sorrow.

It was early still; he was alone in the sanctuary. There was still time.

He continued his slow and stately walk down the aisle, making his way to the *bima*, draped in heavy white cloth in honor of the day. He paused in front of the Ark, nodding his respect, and carefully placed his notebooks on the dais side by side. One book was tattered and dog-eared, obviously well-used. It was thick, at least an inch or so of thin paper, no longer blank. The other was also tattered and worn, and perhaps double the size of the first - two inches at least of thin paper, small, cramped handwriting filling both sides.

The man placed one hand on the first book, lifted his face, and said clearly: "Ok, God. Here are my sins for this year. I confess them, and am sorry for them, and have asked forgiveness for them. I'm here, to make *t'shuvah*, and ask Your forgiveness for the sins I have committed against You." He was silent for a moment, obviously having a private conversation with God.

When he was done, he placed his hand on the second, thicker book. In a clear voice, he spoke again: "And here, God, are your sins. Let's talk..."

Justice, justice shall we all pursue.

Learn

A conversation, heard almost daily in my house when I was a kid:

Mom: Stacey, you know why they don't send donkeys to college, don't you?

Me (after much eye rolling and shaking of the head for the sheer inanity of the response that was sure to come. And a deep, teen-aged sigh of resigned disdain, which actually preceded most statements that I made between the ages of 12 and, um - a lot later in my life).: No, Mom. Why? (sigh)

Mom: Because nobody likes a smart ass.

Ha ha. Said no one, ever - not in response to *that* joke. And it was a joke. Right? I'm going with yes: it was, if nothing else, an attempt.

Thing is, I *was* a smart ass. I was cocky, condescending, sometimes downright mean and obnoxious in my know-it-allness. I was way too smart for my own good. No one, least of all my mother, could teach me anything.

I stayed a smart ass for a long time. I thought of it as protective coloring: I lashed out with my tongue, my rapier wit, that cut with laser precision, drawing blood and leaving scars, all as a way to push you away faster than you could hurt me. Because if there was one thing I had learned, in my short decade or so, it was that you would hurt me. You would crush me and leave me in the dust. In a heartbeat. So the extension of that great piece of learning: push everyone away, as fast as you can. Make them hurt as much as you do.

I was so very wise for a ten year old. Fifteen. Twenty-three. And on and on. I was so wise that I learned absolutely nothing.

Don't get me wrong - I learned a lot of facts. I was pretty gifted in school. I went to college for free on a merit scholarship. Got a full fellowship to grad school, to work on a PhD in Early Modern English history. This does *not* roll off the tongue with any grace or ease. I used that as a wry excuse for quitting the program after a year and a half. That was much easier than admitting another great learning of mine: that I was a fraud - at life, at being a student - at being a human being - and if I didn't quit, and run, and hide, Someone would find out. I have no idea what would have happened if Someone - whomever that was - did "find out;" I just knew it would be bad. Maybe I'd get kicked out of school. Maybe I'd get kicked out of life.

So I did what I had learned to do best. I quit. I left. I hid under a suit of armor that protected me from all the slings and arrows that life had to offer.

I hid for years. Mostly, I hid inside a bottle. Alcohol blotted everything out, but every once in a while, I had to come up for air. So I hid inside the armor of a fiery-eyed activist, working for peace, organizing for justice. I hid inside a tailored suit, selling stuff with a silver tongue, using my words to draw pictures of need and desire. Even after I got sober, and crawled out of the bottle and into the light, I still hid - in work, in marriage. In God. Even that - I loved the community, the holiness and the life of the synagogue. I loved the struggle and the dance with God. But I hid there just the same.

I hid, because it was what I had learned. What I knew. What felt safe.

I still hide. It still feels like the safest bet to me, and I am desperate to feel safe. I still wear my protective armor day in and day out. I may be old-plus-three, but all those lessons learned still run deep. Bottomless pit deep. I'm like the broken kid who can watch everyone else running and playing and just *being*, only from the sidelines, resigned to loneliness, but oh! so very wistful.

I've noticed though, that there a few cracks in the armor. And God, it is getting so heavy. And I am so weary. And I would love nothing more than to say that, for every crack or fissure in that damned armor, some old lesson dies, or escapes, or maybe gets buried, and I learn something new. I learn a different way to be. I learn to live life unguarded. Unprotected. I fear there is no symmetry in this.

I am no longer the condescending, derisive, smart-assed kid who knows everything and so can learn nothing. Thank God. But I don't trust the other lessons much - the lessons on hope, or kindness or love. I am learning them. Painfully slowly, true, but I am learning.

I learned - am learning - to live a sober life. A life without *having* to pick up a drink to be able to get through the next hour, the next minute, the next bit of eternity. I learned - am learning - to seek God. I am not promised that I will ever find God, but that is not the point. I am learning that the joy and the grace are found in the quest. I learned - am learning - that love does not have to be (and should not be) conditional. I learned - am learning, and I find I face this lesson again and again - that, broken as I am, weary as I am, lost and hidden as I am - I am (just maybe) enough.

Leave

"Get out. Leave. Walk away, and don't stop until I tell you to stop." This is how I imagine God's speech to Abraham. back when Abraham was still working in his father's idol shop in the land of Ur. Regardless of the actual Hebrew - or Aramaic - or whatever Urish language they spoke when Ur was the Hot Address of the Fertile Crescent.

Get out, says God, and miracle of miracles - Abraham does. He packs up lock, stock, and ass, and heads west, never looking back. Apparently, he got the memo on the dangers of looking back that some of his in-laws never did.

I cannot imagine the sheer amount of faith that act took. Talk about praying with your feet! On the strength of a voice alone, not even a vision, Abe believed that he would be carried through, be made great. He was picked, chosen, The Man. He never doubted. He argued. He bargained. He obeyed. But he didn't doubt. And he left.

Flash forward a millennium or two, to the Children of Israel. Refugees turned invited guest turned slave over the course of four hundred years. And now, after having their cries of anguish ignored by their God for the whole time, some felon-on-the-run, some Jew-turned-Egyptian-prince-turned-Jew, who had hidden out with the Midianites, marrying a local girl and spending his days herding flocks and talking to bushes - this guy came and started stirring things up and making impossible demands. "Let my people go!" he said to Pharaoh. And Pharaoh seemed to listen - but Pharaoh had his doubts. Pharaoh needed a little proof, a small demonstration of might and power. Pharaoh needed to be shown this might and power again and again times ten.

And finally, after all the blood and frogs and vermin and death stuff, miracle of miracles - Pharaoh said yes. And Moshe said "Get out. Leave. Walk away. Follow me, God'll keep you safe." Their faith was a little more tenuous than Abe's had been, a little more wishy-washy. It was all well and good when they could see the pillar of fire and the cloud of smoke. Absent that, there were a few (how to put this delicately?) blind spots. None of them escaped unscathed, not even Moshe. They were a fiery, tempestuous, argumentative and whiny bunch of people. Once they were slaves, now they were... hungry and tired and scared. *Free* was low on the list of adjectives that they cared about.

But for all of that, they did it: they went. They left the only place they knew as home, the only life they knew how to live, and they did it on the strength of a voice, a vision and a promise. Perhaps not as purposefully as Abraham and his entourage, perhaps a little more frantic than Abe's earlier departure, perhaps they looked back a time or two - but they left.

I think about these scenes - of wonder and chaos and reverence. I think about the faith it took to move. To do the unimaginable: leave. Wow (I know - I'm a writer, I should have more words, better words than this, but, I mean - really: wow!).

I talk about having faith. I *live* on my faith. I get a spiritual high from my faith. Blah blah blah. It's all well and good, until I have to *depend* on my faith, and do the unimaginable - leave. Or, more precisely, leave things behind. I carry everything with me as I traverse my own wilderness - my fear, my doubt, my brokenness. I mean to leave it behind. I really, really do. I *think* I leave behind me, at whatever stopping off place, whatever oasis I find refuge. Imagine my surprise to find that it's all still there, tucked away in some corner of my basket, with all my other stuff. No matter how many times I am shown that I will be carried through, that I will be okay (not that bad things won't ever happen, but that my faith will be strong enough to allow me to put one foot in front of the other, so that I can face whatever is in front of me). No matter, like Pharaoh, I have my doubts. I need to be shown. Again.

I like to think that, even if I haven't quite managed to leave my broken stuff behind, to let it go for good, then at least it's not as big, not as monumentally huge and all-consuming as when I first picked whatever-it-is up, drew it to me and made it grow and blossom (like deadly nightshade). I think, sometimes, that is true. All of those bits of brokenness are smaller, less powerful. They no longer paralyze me, they merely make me stumble.

And this year, as I stand once again at the border of the desert, suddenly freed and commanded to leave - perhaps I will finally have the faith of Abraham and Moshe and the whiny, courageous and human folk of the Exodus. Perhaps I will finally have the faith to leave.

Mercy

I visited my cousin Larry (z"l) one afternoon on my lunch hour, when he lay in the hospital, recovering from brain surgery. He had a brain tumor. It was slowly killing him. It was as if he was on the losing side of a war of attrition: with lightening strike precision, the tumor took away everything meaningful, all the parts of his life and his soul that made him *him*. If it was painful for us, the people who loved him, to watch, what must it have been like for him, to see everything slip away and be powerless to save anything?

There were complications with his last surgery. How could there not be? He had been engaged in battle for twenty long and hard years. He was tired. His body was exhausted. His soul was stretched thin. The doctors induced a coma, in hopes this his body would repair itself, that he would find rest and healing. It was a lovely hope.

They forgot to tell his pain their plan.

Even in a coma, pain ravaged his body. I watched the pain spasm throughout his body, making him writhe. When the spasm passed, he still moved restlessly, unable to find a place where the pain didn't live in him.

My uncle, his father, sat beside him, watching. A completely different flavor of powerless, and just as cruel. He watched his son; I watched my uncle. He felt every bit of Larry's pain. I saw it in his face, in the tension of his body that seemed to echo each spasm. I knew he would take Larry's pain away if he could, take it into himself if he could, if it would give Larry any respite.

The machines whirred in steady rhythm, a strange harmony to Larry's fitful moans. My uncle sat, in an unmoving vigil, a witness. Willing. Watching. Perhaps praying, perhaps cursing. Probably a little of both. Time stretched. It slowed; it may have stopped at one point.

Finally, my uncle shifted. He reached out his hand to touch Larry - soothe him, comfort him, connect in a very real and visceral way. Helplessly hoping - no harlequin romance, but his motion - focused, slow, gentle - his whole body was a prayer.

And he couldn't. He couldn't touch his son, stroke his son's fevered skin. He was terrified that he would cause more pain. But his prayer was in motion already. Raw and naked and filled with absolute love, his body was a prayer.

So he lifted his hand and held it, *closerthanbreath* away from his son, an almost-touch. He held out his hand, afraid, desperate, his sorrow and love so present in that darkened room.

Grace then. A gift. Mercy.

He held out his hand, an aching, almost touch, caressing the space *closerthanthis* away from his son's body, and Larry stilled. His restless, pain-wracked body quieted. My uncle held out his hand, a prayer, a benediction, a blessing. Love. It was all he had to offer. It was enough. Mercy could not bring healing, but there was comfort there, there was rest there. There was love and there was God.

And that was enough.

Peace

I found this quote yesterday while wandering online, wondering whatinhell I was going to say about today's prompt.

"Worrying doesn't take away tomorrow's trouble; it takes away today's peace."

Score one for a God moment - those little bits of happenstance that just seem to fit perfectly when you least expect it. They are unexplainable, and certainly, more rationale folks would just chalk it up to coincidence - and in my more guarded, rational and cynical moments, I do just that. Every once in a while, the mystic in me peeks out from behind the curtains, thumb to nose and tongue out, laughing. What's a girl to do?

Oh yeah: not worry about it.

It has taken me decades to be okay with inconsistency. Add "not knowing" to that short list, along with inexplicable God moments and a Chicagoan's penchant for the Cubs over the White Sox. I may not understand it, but it no longer keeps me up at night, worrying it over like a dog with a bone, chewing and tugging and growling, getting all worked up about nothing. Or everything. Or something - some vague, guessed at thing that may or may not be relevant, or fixable, or preventable, or important. Or anything.

There was a time I would grab onto any of that - calamity real or imagined, rumor innuendo - grab it and worry it and hold on for dear life. I would have entire conversations in my head; hell, I would have multi-user conference calls in there, absolutely independent of any other participants. I knew what you would say to whatever I would say, and then skip six steps ahead, and then six more.

I had all the answers: mine, yours, right, imagined, made up. All of them. What I did not have was any sense of serenity or peace.

I was jumpy and jittery, a bundle of not-so-free floating anxiety. Fix, manage and control - these were my watchwords. Thing is, I would try to do all of that with ideas and situations and things that couldn't be fixed or managed or controlled. At least, not by me.

I've said it before, and it bears saying again: pray to God but row towards shore. Take action. Plan and prepare and put things in motion. Then get out of the way. Breathe. Pause. Think. Ask. Consider. These are generally the next right things to do.

And when I do this, when I get out of my own way, I am blessed with peace. Not that everything works the way I want it to. Not that the results are always happy and good. That's a fairy tale world that I no longer try to live in (mostly).

No, the peace and calm and quiet are what get me through all the other stuff. I don't need to live from crisis to crisis. I can live passionately, fully, joyously, with peace at my core. I can carry that peace with me as I go out to tackle the real work of creating peace in the world and fixing the broken places.

Pray

I start with the premise that it's all Torah. All of it, all of us - we are all wrapped in the scrolls of Torah, playing out the glory of life. And because it's all Torah, I take my truth wherever I find it. I find it everywhere (after all, everywhere *is* Torah, right?) I just need to notice it, recognize it.

A bunch of years ago, I was locked in fierce combat while angels danced across ladders and I dreamed of God and slept on a rock-strewn bed. The battle raged for a small slice of forever. Sometimes I danced with the angels, sometimes I wrestled with God. It all but consumed me.

And then: truth. Just like. Truth and I slept and did not dream and found the gates of heaven, and finally knew they'd been there all along.

Truth then (and now, because this remains the most profound truth I have ever kept, and it has changed my life forever) came from a movie. *Shadowlands*, to be exact. It's a great movie about the author of the Narnia books (and others), a flawed man who finds love, and God, and himself. See it, if you haven't. I will not bore you with the details, except to share one scene. C.S. Lewis is leaving his wife's hospital bed. She is dying, and he is bereft. He meets a few colleagues, Oxford dons like himself, who, in a singular act of cruelty and contempt, stop Lewis - who had made a name for himself as a charismatic Christian, giving lectures throughout England with the basic premise "everything happens because God made it so; therefore, *anything* that happens *must* be good and right - and ask (in effect) "How's that prayer thing working for you now?" Lewis looks up at them, and with profound sadness and weariness, says "Prayer doesn't change God. Prayer changes me."

That simple statement may have saved my life. It certainly changed my life, and changed my relationship to prayer and God.

When I pray, I open myself up to hearing answers and finding comfort.

How do I know this works? Not long ago, at morning Shabbat services, I had a tantrum. Not attractive in a woman who is old plus two. People were not behaving the way I thought they should. People were disturbing my prayer, my service, my time with God and the soft, golden light of a Saturday morning. I had, as it were, a fit of pique.

One woman, in particular, was pressing every button, standing on every nerve. This is not new. She is old and mean and demands to be the center of attention, even in the middle of a service. That week's Torah portion was filled with blessings and curses. I was cursing plenty. And then, in the middle of the *Amidah* (the silent part), I remembered that this week's Torah portion also reflects on a prayer - for a heart that knows and eyes that see. So I prayed differently today, and asked for an open heart.

And this is what I saw: an old woman, alone and in desperate, perhaps hopeless, spiritual pain. So much so that all she can give to her community is a portion of that pain. How incredibly sad - to be looked at with pity and disdain by your chosen community. And as so often happens, my prayer did not change God, but, when I ask and seek with even the slightest bit of humility and humanity - my prayer changes me.

As a result, in the middle of the *Amidah*, I went from petulant child to something quite different - I am trying to understand what we as a community, what I as a part of that community, can do to ease her pain. I know that I cannot fix her. That's not my job. But how do I respond to her and her pain? How do I satisfy my need to pray and connect in the face of her rage and despair?

I'm not trying to be codependent about this, but there has to be a balance - doesn't there? True, she is disruptive and explosive, she will not listen; nor does she (apparently) care what her actions do to the flow of the service. It is also clear, I think, that she feels apart from, separated from. She feels that she is The Other, the stranger in our midst. We are commanded to remember the stranger, for we were strangers once. We are commanded to care for the stranger, for he is us.

I fear I did not act very Jewishly in this. I fear I did not act very humanly - or maybe the problem is that I acted all too humanly. I will pray, and be changed, and I will hear the voice of God. And I will know, when I ask for a heart that knows and eyes that see, I will reach out, *b'tzelem elohim* - in the image of God - and make a holy space next to me for everyone, even this bitter woman, this stranger who is, after all, me.

Ready

I am not ready. I'm not close to being prepared. Life. Work. This day. Not this week nor next. Not ready for parenting (don't even get me started on parenting (let alone single parenting). I would need to climb a very tall ladder to get to the ground floor of unprepared in parenting). I'm so unprepared that this essay was due yesterday. It is now 9:13pm on the sixth of Nisan (though given the Hebrew division of days, it's probably the seventh of Nisan. Oy.).

I have good intentions. I have plans. I make lists. I talk - out loud, in my head, alone or in groups - I understand the concept. Really and truly, I get how much easier, how much smoother life flows when I am prepared. I may even have experienced the whole prepared thing once or twice, somewhere along the line. It felt - good. Right. It all *just fits*.

Mostly though, I'm the one who hasn't read the instructions; the one who's forgotten to print the presentation on the day of the big meeting; the one still cleaning the living room even as the doorbell rings. I am grateful for convenience stores in airports, so that I can buy the eleventy-seven items I managed to forget. I would continue in this tirade, but I was running late and left all my notes sitting on the kitchen counter. Or in my car. I think.

Mostly I spend my life winging it. I have become the Master of the Ad Lib, the Queen of Last Minute Projects and Cramming. I can hit the target 98% of the time when shooting from the hip.

I am NOT ready. Ever. I am not prepared.

So what?

What difference does it make if I'm prepared or not? I'm not hurting anyone. Well - not really. I'm the one who is frazzled. It is my life that's in (total) disarray. I am not a Boy Scout (for several obvious reasons), although I was a Girl Scout, but I was a horrible and unprepared Girl Scout, if preparedness is even a thing for them.

So what?

It's Passover. Or close to it. It's the season, the celebration of our redemption. And there is something important, something sacred and holy about preparing for these days.

As I begin with the physical tasks of preparation - cleaning out the cabinets, polishing the silver, figuring out the menu (because all of that is part of the holiness of preparation) all of that creates a shift - from the physical to the spiritual. I am changed. I move into a slightly different rhythm. There is a purpose, a mindfulness, a thoughtfulness that washes over me, so that I become ready for Passover - not just my house, but my heart.

I don't always finish the physical stuff, the cleaning and polishing, the cooking. I'm still, you know, me. Chances are I will have started late, with no real plan in mind, other than some vague, inchoate and amorphous idea that I should host a Seder and invite a bunch of people.

But my heart - my heart changes, quiets, is so much more present. And it changes enough, exactly enough, for me to enter into that holy and sacred place joyously, mindfully grateful that once we were slaves now we are free.

See

Earlier this year, I was afraid that I was going blind. Sorry. Wrong. No. I wasn't afraid. Afraid is for spiders or the dark. Heights (or, in my case, falling, which I think is a much more healthy and realistic fear). Lots of things to merely fear.

I have retinopathy. Proliferative retinopathy, to be exact. In layman's terms, I have bleeding in my eyes. Both of them. Every once in a while, the veins leak. Blood seeps, forming what I like to call little paramecium branches waving in front of my line of sight, making it difficult to see. I have laser surgery to cauterize the veins, and voila! I can mostly see. One morning, last summer, I woke up and it was as if someone had taken a gob of Vaseline and smeared it across my right eye. I could see color and light. That was it.
Shape escaped me, except in some vague, amorphous way.

What I felt wasn't fear, a walk in the park, that get shivers in the dark the test is today? kind of thing. This was absolute terror. This was oh my God what will I do if I can't see? This hits everything. I'm a single mom. I drove to work, drove to visit clients, drove everywhere. My job depended upon hours and hours in front of a computer screen, analyzing data stored in teeny, tiny little Excel cells that were getting harder and harder to see, even when I blew them up. Large. The less contrast there was, the less chance I could see. On grey days, on the gray streets with the silver cars and a fine mist of rain, I was lost. In the dark, almost literally. I grounded myself from driving at night altogether. And did I mention that I'm a single mom? And a writer. What the hell? How could I write how could I take care of my son if I couldn't see?

I am making this so complicated.

I keep adding strings of words and thoughts and twisting them into some weird tapestry that, in my head is all clean lines and distinct colors: ordered, measured. One could even say, stately and fine. On the screen, it is squiggles of black, with occasional blotches that smudge and hide whatever lines of text it is that keep spilling, end over end, world without end, amen.

Ugh.

Here's the deal: I am terrified that I am going blind, that I will lose the ability to see.

It is a real, though perhaps unlikely, fear. I have a handful of health conditions, all related, all requiring specialists and special attention. And one of those conditions is an eye thing. As a result, I have a retina guy. I have an eye guy. I get lasered and treated and operated on every so often. It is controlled, my condition, but barely. It is progressive, they tell me. It will probably get worse.

And from there, from here, this simple, solid spot, I spin - a whirlpool of dark and limitless power that sucks and pulls and consumes all of the light, all of the hope...

See? Even when I stop (try to stop) the spilling and spinning, the anguish and the angst - they seep into this simple thing: I am terrified that I am going blind.

How will I see the color red? Or that single line of light that separates the sky from the sea? How will I see the messiness amid the grandeur - for every fiery sunset, For every sky stained scarlet and gold, that makes you breathless with wonder and awe, there is a river choked by sludge, or a village ravaged by war and poverty.

How will I see my words, put them into their proper order, see their rhythm and flow?

How will I see the words of Torah, painstakingly, lovingly drawn in their regulated sameness, row upon row upon column and page, so that even the mistakes are present and made beautiful, and every single scroll, every single scribe for millennia has infused his own spirit, his soul into those letters? How will I see to chant those words that fill me and still me and baffle me? This is the offering I give- will it be my sacrifice?

How will I see my son's face, watch him grow and change and become all of the things that I can just glimpse now, the strength and compassion and hardness and surety, all of those amazing things that have been germinating and are now just beginning to show? How in the world will I see this beautiful boy become a man if I am blind?

Every morning, we give thanks to God who opens the eyes of the blind. I do not have this faith. I believe in the metaphor of this prayer. I fear though, that I am going blind.

Trust

Trust.

Ugh. Son of a bitch. Fifty-three, and I still only mostly trust the bad stuff. The good stuff, the stuff I don't trust, when that happens, it's always a surprise. Even so, I wait for the other shoe to drop. Sometimes I feel as if I am walking through a minefield only I can see. The traps are many and deadly, and their placement has no rhyme or reason.

Nowhere is safe.

I'd like to say that it's gotten better. And you know, at times, it has. There are times when my faith fairly pulses with life, when I fit inside my own skin and my own head, when I am not hungry or angry or lonely or tired - it is infinitely better then. I trust. Not just that the good stuff will happen, but that the bad stuff most likely won't. Or, that even if the bad stuff does, or the good stuff doesn't, it's still all good. Because that's just stuff that happens around me. It' isn't me. It is not God's cosmic party joke of pulling the rug out from underneath my feet like the bad magician does to the tablecloth. It's not karma, payback for sins real and imagined (and trust me: I have an *awesome* imagination).

Stuff happens. Or doesn't. And life continues, in all its glory and joy and pain and wonder and delight.

Like I said, this is me, on a good day.

Me on a bad day? Minefield, laced with quicksand and evil spells. And faith that is, if not absent, infinitely small. And while I would love to live in the drama of woe-is-me, this is Elul, and so I am called to right-size my life, my belief, my thoughts and fears. Small as that faith is, microscopic, and if it were sound it would be pitched so that only dogs could hear it - it is enough.

You get the picture. My faith shrinks. And my ability to trust - really trust. not just wait for the horrors of life to visit themselves upon me - is directly proportional to that faith. Here's the curious thing though. Even when I am stuck in that waiting line of dread, I can step back. I can, disconnectedly and dispassionately get out of the way and leap.

Sometimes, life is hard. And you're afraid. I am; you may not be. Or you're - I am - tired, and a little lost, and kinda broken and lonely and maybe you skipped lunch and the noise was too loud and the damn air conditioner broke - or not. It could just be one of those beautiful, sunny, blessedly cool and non-humid days, and the sky is a liquid blue and everything is just going right. Sometimes it's one of those days.

And you're asked - I'm asked - to trust. Something. Someone. Some Deity. And I freeze. And I can't. And my faith has taken a powder and I am defenseless in a very scary world.

But you do it anyway. You leap. I leap, as if the dogs of hell were nipping at my heels, or sometimes I just stumble and fall forward-ish. But I trust anyway, because I know, even if I can't feel it in that moment, that I will be okay. I will be caught and carried and held, safe. I will not always get the Good Stuff. The bad stuff of trust will still happen.

As Stephen Sondheim said, "Well, now you know. People love you and tell you lies. Now you know."

But I do it anyway - trust. I suck it up, screw my courage to the sticking post and get out of the way. And life goes on. And good stuff happens. And bad stuff. And I stumble around, almost blind, and just when I'm absolutely certain that I will fall - fail - there is a hand to hold me up and help me along my way.

Understand

Way back in the 80s, when most of my friends were enjoying the excesses of the Reagan years (for the second time) (and trust, me I never understood the Reagan years the *first* time around; the second set had me reeling).

While my friends were out merging and acquiring and amassing small to medium fortunes, I took a sharp left turn, quit graduate school (and the full fellowship that had been attached to my acceptance) and became a political activist. Or, as my parents still say - I became a professional beggar and street walker. Really, I went to work for ACORN: the Association of Community Organizations for Reform Now. It was long before it had become a dirty word, long before the Tea Partiers t-bagged it. In fact, it was way long before social activism and social justice were once again in vogue, having been placed in mothballs somewhen in the 70s.

I loved it. It filled me with purpose - I got to do good, every day. I was changing the world, every day, one stop sign, one signature, one voice at a time. I made next to no money. One of the unspoken ideals of the organization was, in order to organize the poor, you have to be poor. I didn't care. There were roommates (all fiery-eyed co-workers who were in the same boat with the same single-minded zeal). There were creative finances. There were parents in a pinch, who clearly were appalled that I'd given up academia, but were willing to let me run with this crazy political thing, hoping it was merely a passing phase, waiting until I met a nice Jewish lawyer, got married and settled down in the suburbs to raise babies, bake cookies and join a country club (not necessarily in that order).

I was in the canvas; we were the fundraisers. While the organizers were out, organizing the poor (or, rousing the rabble as my parents were wont to say) I was out, pounding the pavement (walking the streets), out in the middle income neighborhoods, gaining support and funds for our work. I raised gobs of money. I moved up the ranks - first to Field Manager, running a crew of canvassers out on "turf", and later, Canvas Director, running an office. We raised thousands of dollars, every night, rain or shine, hot or cold, five days a week.

I was on fire. I was so alive then!

As you might guess, staff turnover was pretty high. I did a lot of recruitment and interviewing. First interview was always a group one. This is how I began the interview, every time:

Is housing a right or a privilege? What about access to medical care? How about heat in the winter or cooling in the summer? Money is power - and without it, you have no power. So how do you change things?

I did not grow up with these questions. Frankly, had you asked me not too many years before my ACORN days, my answers may have surprised you. Even so - I pass that off as youthful naiveté. By the time I became an adult - a thinking, caring, reasoning adult, I had a whole different set of values, and a whole different understanding of the world and how it works.

I bring all this up because the prompt for 16 Elul is Understand. And I have to say - I don't. I didn't 30 years ago, and I don't today.

I don't understand how anyone can believe that we do not have a responsibility to make sure that people have a safe place to live- all people: people we love, people we know, people we don't like, people who don't like us. We have abandoned buildings everywhere, and abandoned people, too. I don't understand how we can tolerate this.

I don't understand how we have some of the most advanced medical technology on the planet, magical drugs, healers, hospitals - and yet we feel justified in saying "You have money, so you deserve to be healed. You do not. Sorry. Keep your fingers crossed." Hoping for the best is not a treatment plan. I don't understand how we can allow people to die - every day - because they can't afford even the most basic of medical care.

I don't understand how we throw out tons of food, literally, when there are people who are starving.

I don't understand so much of what seems to drive our society here in the States. Of course, I don't seem to understand so much of what drives society in the world at large, either. As cynical as I am - or pass myself off to be - I am still so damned naive. I don't understand hatred. I don't understand bigotry. I don't understand sexism, homophobia, indifference. I don't understand war or corruption.

I just don't.

We read in the Torah: "There shall be no needy." And just in case we let something slip through the cracks and there *was* some needy person, we were commanded to give the needy person whatever it was they needed, freely, graciously. Don't believe in God? No problem - do all of this, demand this, because it is the right thing, the human thing to do. How can it not be that?

If you had to look someone in the eye and say - sorry, no food for you; no house; no care; no money; no voice; no life - could you? Not to the masses, but to a single person, standing before you, asking for help - could you turn that person away, condemn him or her to death?

We cannot stand idly by while there is want or need. *We cannot.* To do so would be to turn our backs on our humanity. We must work for a world in which there are no needy. Here's what I understand today, without any hesitation - What's expected of me, of humanity? Seek justice, love mercy and kindness, walk humbly with God.

Wonder

For the past year, give or take, I have been wishing people a year filled with wonder in my Facebook birthday message. I tend to gloss over the exact meaning of that. It sounds good: deep, kind of profound, definitely spiritual in some way, and certainly with a vague and unspoken reference to God. In actuality, I don't know that I've ever given any real thought to what a year of wonder actually means.

As I was mulling over this topic today, I tried a couple of meanings on for size. Given that I am convinced I have ADD, my meanderings have been

Oh look! Squirrels! And bright, shiny objects! Detours...

As I started to say, before I interrupted myself back there-- my meanderings have been interesting. That one of them was "I wonder how I have managed to not kill my beloved boy child yet///" will give you an idea of just how far afield (and how much on the edge) I can get. My son, though, gets me closer to an answer, a better understanding of wonder.

We were sitting in services this morning, me because I wanted to be there, he because I forced him out of bed and insisted, He's a good kid, so my insistence was not too demanding. He sat next to me, playing with the tzitzit of my tallit, listening some, fiddling some, reading some, possibly praying some. Later, after the service, sitting and kibbitzing with friends, my son informed me, again, that he didn't believe in God. And again, I answered him in the only way that makes sense to me; "That's okay; you believe in kindness. I'm okay with that."

This being the time of year that it is, I felt the need to elaborate. "Nate, you look out at the woods there behind the house and see nature in all its glory-- fractals and delicate equations and chemical reactions and set laws that are knowable and predictable. I see all that, my beloved boy, and hovering just above that field, I see God. You say science; I say God. I don't think God cares one way or another what you call Him (Her)."

What is that leap? How do I get to God-- the God of fractals and predictable science? We both looked at that idyllic scene with a sense of wonder. I think though, the wonder of it all, is the willingness to strip bare-- leave the cynicism and absolute certainty off to the side. There is delight in wonder, and surprise. There is something breathtaking about it. Perhaps the difference between my son's vision and mine is that I see no disconnect between science and God.

I want to end here. Mostly. I don't know that I'm quite satisfied with this explanation. There is some otherness that pushes one into wonder. There is a willingness to be vulnerable and naked-- a willingness to disallow preconceived ideas of how things work/ There should be a sense of God, of beyondness. And I know I'm making up words, but I'm trying to pull this together and the words I know aren't getting me far enough.

Wonder is a startlement, a gasp of recognition and beauty. It is God and fractals and a double helix, twined in an intimate dance. It is a leap, from a field of liquid green laced with late summer gold to a glorious hymn to God, made of bright color and soft breezes.

And all of this may be true, but it doesn't even come close to the sense that is wonder. But there's this-- I went to service with my son this morning. I, because I wanted to; he because I insisted. And there was enough love, enough trust, enough a sense of rightness and respect, that we sat, for an hour or two, praying, listening, fiddling, laughing and loving. For all the geometry and beyondness: there is breathtaking wonder in that simple and glorious moment.

Endings and Beginnings

The Faith of Return

I've said it before – how awesome is it, that before God ever created the heavens and the earth, God created t'shuvah – return. So we end, and begin, and end again, ever and always. And in between, we learn and change and love and dare and leap and laugh. We put one foot in front of the other, walking through the wilderness, and if we're lucky, if we have faith, if we are ready to see, we find a few hands to hold, a few lights to shine on the narrow path we walk.

If we're lucky, we realize, even in our fear, there is hope. In our loneliness, we are surrounded by love. In our doubt, we dance – with infinite grace – in the palm of God's hand.

We gathered here, Together,
at the edge, bathed in silence
and bending light,
weary and ready, to leap.
To dive into that pool filled to overflowing
with love and doubt and hunger and hope,
and stars that reel in mirrored waters.
And so I leap with the
light of Heaven, of earth and sky,
Reflecting all my doubt
my love and longing.
There is beauty in my pain.
There is more in Letting go.
And so I breathe:
I am returned
To the edge of my
Beginning.

Return

So, here's the part where I get a little wonky, a little out there. A little (if I may be so bold) *vulnerable.* Here's the part where I say:

We are *always* at the Gate.

We are *always* at Sinai.

We are *always* redeemed.

We all - every one of us - walk a path with God. We may not recognize it or acknowledge it, but we do. There is beauty and pain and hope and despair in every one of those paths. Percentages may change. How long I choose to walk in despair may change and shift. It is the same for sorrow and wonder and joy. They are all there. It's what we carry and what we take away. It is our breath. Our souls. Our hope and sorrow. It is the Gate. It is Sinai.

It is, ever and always, our redemption.

The beauty of Elul is the realization that I am there - *right there* - poised at the edge of everything - always. I have dived and reflected, shined lights and prepared, to stand here - right here - with my heart open , eyes wide, filled with blessings and forgiveness, filled with my humanity and acceptance of yours. Ready, so very ready, to step through. To fit, to be, to become.

Ready.

And the thing I take away from this holy and sacred undertaking (entered into on a lark, carried out reluctantly, resentful of the discipline and formality, and doing it anyway) (and learning and growing and becoming as a result) - another of those profound, transformative, life-altering truths that I find unlooked for and in odd places - what I find is this: *either every day is holy or no day is.* Today, I choose to live in a world where every day is holy. The gate is always open. I am always there. God is always there, ready to catch me, grab my hand and dance.

Tonight. Tomorrow. Yom Kippur. A week from next Thursday. Either every day is holy or no day is. The gates of repentance are always open. I am returned. I am redeemed. *All I have to do is step through.*

Epilogue

More Questions than Answers

A few years ago, on the first Sunday of religious school, I challenged my seventh grade students: "How do you have a conversation with God in the 21st century? Do you even have a conversation at all? How do you come to God when life is good? More, how do you come to God in times of anger or sadness or despair, when all you want to do is curse at God? How do you connect to Judaism?"

Being a fan of symmetry and neatly wrapped boxes, on the last Sunday of the year, I asked them: "What is it that connects you? To Judaism, to God? *Are* you connected? What does it mean, to be a Jew?"

I don't know that I have answers any more now than I did when I started that year. For that matter, any more than I did when I lost God, when I was convinced that God had lost me, or any more than when I felt sheltered and carried gently in the palm of God's hand. But I know now, I think, what connects me. I know, now, what binds me to my faith.

But still I ask myself *"Have I done enough? Have I, have we, the community that surrounds and supports these questing, growing, questioning minds - have we given them enough, to anchor them in their doubt and disbelief, to strengthen them in their journey to adulthood? Will they, too, become Jews by choice?"*

I look at my son, who, at sixteen, is *right there:* a jumble of belief and doubt and cynicism and hope, so ready to believe, so fearful of his honest disbelief. What can I give him, that he will choose to be a Jew? Around and around I go, on a merry-go-round of ask-and-answer. And every so often, I'm lucky enough to stop long enough to hear enough from others who ride their own merry-go-rounds of hope and doubt and faith and love.

It lets me know, if nothing else, that I'm asking the right questions. At least, that we are all asking a lot of the same questions. And we're finding some... if not *answers*, then at least a little bit of clarity. And so I can ask: what does it take to be enough? And I can start to hear the tin calliope merry-go-round music of an answer coming back to me:

It's about passion, I think. My passion. Our passion. The passion and joy and exuberance of being Jewish: of study and community and service and prayer and family and God. It's choosing and being engaged in the choice. It's mindful and sometimes hard and sometimes frustrating and always, always - *it's ok to be passionate*. It's good to find the wonder and sense the awe of who we are and where we fit. Judaism can be an intellectual pursuit. But it is so much more; can be so much more. If we allow it. If we let it. How can we not show that? How can we not share that?

But wait - there's more. It's also about obligation. We spend so much time sheltering our young, giving and teaching and doing for them, and we don't always remember to teach them their obligation to us, their community. We don't always show them that there is as much joy, as much passion in obligation and service outwards as there is in being served. God has taught us that lesson well: we are commanded to serve, we are bound by our obligations one to another, to our community and to God. It is that obligation that helps give us all a framework of connection that can transcend doubt or disbelief.

[handwritten margin note: I forgot to include myself in teaching this on]

Passion. Obligation. Joy. God. Beginning the conversation. Being caught in the act - of choosing, every day, to be a Jew. What else, what else, what else? What am I missing? What are we missing? I don't know it all, not by a long shot. But I've learned that there are those who can fill in the blanks, if I ask. There are those who can help me find the questions, if I listen.

So - I'm listening. I'm asking. Is it enough? Is there joy enough, wonder enough to bridge the doubt? What connects us? What will bind us, one to another and to God? What words do I give to my son, so that he can find his own way to choose, every day, to be a Jew?

And finally, I offer a small prayer of my own: that we can all listen in wonder, ask in joy, choose in faith, dance with God.

Amen.

Thank you for being a part of my journey. Thank you for shining your lights in my darkness, for celebrating my joy and triumph, for teaching me the glory of silence, the holiness of community. You brought your songs, your souls, your lives and have given me welcome.

I have been blessed beyond imagining.

Good prayer
for community
Shabbas dinner

Copyrights

All essays and poems originally published electronically on *Stumbling Towards Meaning* (http://staceyzrobinson.blogspot.com), as noted below:

Joy in the Empty Spaces	c 2011
A Quiet and Holy Current	c 2014
A Cry in the Wilderness	c 2012
The Sound of Your Voice (Originally published as "Hear")	c 2014
Blessing and Pain (Originally published as "Bless")	c 2014
Week's End, with a Promise	c 2009
The Holiness of Separation	c 2012
Psalm 92	c 2010
Friday Night Kitchen	c 2011
And When I Leave	c 2014
Fear, Faith and a Really Big Sea	c 2011
Opening the Door	c 2012
The Holiness of Silence	c 2014
What I Brought	c 2013
An Absence of Color and Light	c 2013
In the Space of T'kiyah	c 2012
War	c 2014
Bound to Freedom (Originally published as "Freedom")	c 2014
Ribbons	c 2011
Twenty Three	c 2014
Be	c 2013
Believe	c 2013
Bless	c 2015
Clean	c 2014
Count	c 2014
Dare	c 2014
End	c 2014
Enslave	c 2014
Fear	c 2013
Forgive	c 2013
Hope	c 2013
Justice	c 2013
Learn	c 2014
Leave	c 2014
Mercy	c 2013
Peace	c 2013
Pray	c 2013

Ready   c 2014
See   c 2014
Trust   c 2014
Understand   c 2014
Wonder   c 2013
Return   c 2013
More Questions than Answers   c 2012

The Sound Between the Notes (22) ✓ Song Unfinished (3:

Printed by Books on Demand GmbH, Norderstedt / Germany